Linda Falcone

If They are Roses

The Italian Way with Words

Draß wishes you a very Merry Christmas and a prosperous New Year.

Sis Spelli!

If They are Roses

The Italian Way with Words

by Linda Falcone

Illustrations, layout and cover design: Leo Cardini, agilelogica.it
Copyediting and proofreading: Ellen Wert, for The Florentine Press, Giovanni Giusti, agilelogica.it
Editorial consultant: Marco Badiani, agilelogica.it

ISBN 978-88-902434-3-1
1°edizione: May 2008
2008 B'Gruppo srl, Prato
Collana The Florentine Press
Riproduzione vietata

Printed by Tipografia La Marina - Calenzano, Firenze

In our efforts to respect the environment, The Florentine Press used eco-friendly paper in the printing of this book.

Contents

Se son rose fioriranno...

Preface

On my 30th birthday, I abandoned a novel I'd been struggling to finish for years. It was a hopeless case and I was suddenly adult enough to admit it. Novel writers need a conflict that's deep enough to bridge the gaps between chapters. If you don't have a conflict, a love interest will do; if you don't have a love interest, then God bless you—there's no need to prolong the agony.

After four years of drafts, I was finally willing to face the facts. My would-be Italian novel had none of the essentials. My conflicts, though excruciating, were about as profound as having to wait in line at the post office. My love interest was a country rather than a person, and, as far as I could see, there was no real resolution to the relationship. And when there's no resolution, you can just kiss your sweet little novel goodbye.

After I bid mine farewell, it took me two years to face the typewriter again. My reconciliation with the written word occurred when my long-time-no-see friend Janelle came back to Florence after a lengthy stay in London. 'Hey, what ever happened to that book you were writing?', she asked when we met for drinks in via del Corso.

'It didn't work,' I told her.

'You mean it didn't work out with the publisher?'

'No, I mean it just didn't work.'

'Well, what does it need?'

'A big pair of scissors, maybe.'

'You know', my friend mused, 'There's a new English-speaking newspaper coming to Florence. Grass-roots. You'd like it. It's in the Oltrarno district and they want 750-word articles on Italy. You should chop off chapter of your book and go talk to them.'

In truth, there is nothing I like more than 'grass-roots.'

So I took Janelle's advice and crossed the river with the right amount of words in tow. Two weeks later I was commissioned to write a bi-weekly column on language and culture in Italy—there was a space on page 15 that needed filling. My initial salary was a desk at the press office near Santo Spirito, and although the job didn't pay the rent, free office space in Florence is worth the whole bank of Monopoly money. Thus, began my frenzied search for the 'word of the week.' Thus began this slightly haphazard collection of stories about Italy.

To me, they are love stories—of the 'for better and for worse' variety. Italy has never tempted me with temporary infatuation; it is the love of my life and the bane of my existence. An incorrigible mix of 'leave me alone' and 'don't ever leave me', my feelings reflect this culture's inherent paradox. Though positively sagging with downfalls, Italy's strengths are nothing short of astounding. And while literature and cinema paint this country in glossy shades of Fantasyland, in real life, it's just that—real life. Cultural survival is a day-to-day effort where admiration, frustration, affection and bewilderment are daily bread.

The stories in this book speak primarily of culture shock and writer's block—my two most faithful suitors. Culture shock encapsulates one's relationship with the world; writer's block reflects one's search for unborn potential. Part threat and part delight, there's no known cure for either.

Thank God. What would life be with nothing to overcome? Resolution is often over-rated. Give me discovery, inconformity, struggle and truce. Give me a good word to follow. And by all means, give me a road that leads to Italy.

Being back

It's Tuesday, the day we put the newspaper to bed. And yes, since the entire staff has spent the last few weeks boldly courting summer, we are surprised that the paper is already pushing so hard to hatch. On most days, our staff forms a relatively perfect union that works in varying levels of peace and harmony. Today, there is little room for love. It's not even midday and we've already fought about a front-page photo no one will ever see, waged a war over headlines no one will ever read, and I've almost been fired for inserting three overlooked commas. Ours is a free press, and last-minute punctuation is very expensive.

I have a language column to write. It has to been signed, proofed and delivered by 3pm and I am by no means as worried as I should be. Sometimes the expression I'll focus on escapes me until just before deadline, but this week, I've been lucky.

The word has followed me every where—chasing me down streets and flitting in and out of everyone's eyes. *Il rientro.* All morning it has been looming over our desks, ominous, carnivorous and invisible. The pressroom door is closed, but it has somehow seeped under the doorway, merciless as the damp.

The first signs of 're-entry' started a few days ago as the familiar snake of traffic began inching wickedly towards the city. That trail of cars brings Italy's actors and actresses back to their everyday stages. September is here; the show is about to begin again. For a month, all of the city's respectable citizens drew the curtain and stayed out of the limelight. That's the privilege of August in Florence. Shops close, shutters shut, everyone turns the key three times and makes a break for mountain peaks or sand dunes. Daily drama flies north for the summer. No one has the strength to argue about things that can't get done anyway.

With September's *rientro*, the spectacle inherent in Italian living once again finds its way to the surface. The lovers, the haters, the smart and the quick, the belligerent, the wily and the wise—all those characters who normally populate the Florentine stage-play—take up their roles once more. For Italians, *il rientro* is another way to say 'Lights, camera, action!' It's time to try and get your way again. In August, you could afford to be slow and low and silent. With *il rientro* you have to be tricky and witty and loud again.

Il rientro is always hard, they say. I, for one, will miss the sea, shushing ladies in floppy hats and sandcastles by the Adriatic's edge. I will miss lukewarm pasta from a thermos and breaded veal cutlets at the beach. But most of all, I will miss the two hours of 'digestion time' Italians call *le ore del silenzio*. From two to four o'clock, protesting children up and down the beach are banished from the seaside and bade to keep quiet and in the shade. In Italy, bathing in salt water after lunch blocks the intestines and paralyzes all major muscle groups. It's simply common knowledge.

During *le ore del silenzio* kids take turns being buried alive. Dying during digestion is not as risky as swimming, and nobody ever scolds them for it. Adults have it much better. We get dibs on all the lounge chairs. We find time to shamelessly snore undisturbed or read a year's worth of 'pink' journalism in a week and a half. We are even allowed to break the *silenzio* to complete crosswords that require group effort.

But speaking of group effort, my colleagues behind me are making absolutely no effort to overcome their unanimous *rientro* grouchiness.

Giacomo is worried about getting the paper to the printer on time, so he is busy finding everything we've done wrong over the past four days. He used to be an architect but always talks like a lawyer when he is feeling cross. 'It is an unarguable fact that this local news article is a mortal bore', Giacomo tells his brother.

'So go throw yourself off Ponte Vecchio. That'll make a good story', comes Marco's reply.

'Yes, but if I dive, then you'll be stuck writing it.'
'You're right. Never mind, *lascia fare*.'

I smile in spite of myself. Unfortunately, they see it. To be happy during the days of *il rientro* is a serious breach in the Florentine Code of Correct Conduct. But I can't help it. I'm happy to be back. I love the quick wit that abounds here and even the pointless bickering that sprouts on 'ruby' Tuesdays.

'What the hell are you so happy about?', Giacomo wants to know. My smile is going to be his next fight.

'I was just thinking of instating an *ore del silenzio* rule here at the office. Anyone who makes a peep during digestion gets buried in quicksand. What do you say? After lunch, silence and detective paperbacks only.'

Evidently the idea is appealing enough to spark Giacomo's grudging interest. 'Would we get to do crosswords too?'

'You know I'd never object to the search for good words.'
'So what's your word of the week, Lovely?'

Italians forget fights as quickly as they start them. 'Lovely' means we are friends again. 'I'm writing about *il rientro*', I tell him.

'*Un articolo triste.* Why such a sad article to start the new season?'

All good drama needs some element of tragedy', I muse. 'What are you saying?' He frowns. 'You're writing an article not a stage play.'

Apparently, this is going to be premise for another argument. Oh well. It is September and time to keep up with the punches. The sweet lull of August fades so quickly. *Il rientro* has burst into town. The city gates stand wide open. The swing and sting of Italian life has re-turned in full force.

The doctor is in

Like many people in Italy, I work several jobs. Every 10 days or so, Boss Number Three calls me. There is an urgent manuscript waiting for me at the translation studio. Can I pick it up? Stay up all night to do it? Bring it by in the morning? Niccolò tells me it's super urgent and then he whines, argues and grovels. The man is always late in asking and I always agree to do it anyway. But only on the condition that he treat me to a *caffè al tavolo* at the Giubbe Rosse upon delivery. It's eight euro for a cappuccino and *brioche* there, and after working under pressure I liked to be treated like an intellectual.

On the morning of our last translation emergency, I stopped by the studio right after a trip to the hairdresser's. She'd given me a pixie cut to go with my 1920s hat, and for all of five minutes I felt fashionable.

In Italy, I can never make the feeling last longer than that. As soon as I walked in the door, my boss cocked his head to one side and studied me. In Italy, employers are allowed to react to their employees' haircuts. I should have been prepared.

'That haircut makes you look like a nine-year-old', he said.

'Nico! That comment would make me a millionaire in any courthouse in America. But, harassment aside, it's not quite the look I was hoping for.'

'How can talking about your haircut be harassment?'

'Because it's my hair and you have no business talking about it.'

'Americans worry about very irrelevant things.'

'Yeah, and Italians say very irrelevant things. Give me the manuscript.'

Unfortunately, however, there must have been some truth in his 'nine-year-old' comment.

Later that day I went apartment hunting. I had a few pre-requisites, I explained to the real estate agent. No student housing. Nothing too centrally located. Reasonably priced and unfurnished, please. In Italy kitchens are not built-in and I needed somewhere to put my sink. I was looking for a place where permanent people lived.

The woman sized me up and apparently thought me to be at least 20 years younger than I am.

'Oh', she said, 'we have a flat here that fits your needs. Unfortunately, the landlord would prefer an adult.'

'An adult? Then, I think I qualify.'

'Oh, no', she corrected herself, 'I mean he wants someone who works. Someone with a salary.'

'Well', I replied, visibly shaken, 'usually, I just work for the glory. But sometimes they pay me.'

At the Giubbe Rosse, I shared my horror story with Niccolò. As is common, his response in no way reflected my pain. The only time Italians are bland is when you could really use a big reaction. The best I got was the off-handed question, 'Did you introduce yourself as *dottoressa*?'

'*Dottoressa*? Of course not. I hate that.'

'Well, if you don't play by the rules, don't complain that the game isn't working for you. In Italy, *è tutto nel titolo*, it's all in the title. When it comes to earning respect in this country, nobility and holiness are best. Education earns you the next step on the social staircase. If you want to be treated well, it's best to use your title. Here it doesn't matter who you are, it matters who you seem. *Dottore* and *dottoressa* demand preferential treatment.'

'Yes, but why should it? Who cares about the fact that I have a stupid university degree? Customer service shouldn't depend on a title. It's for snobs and I hate it.'

Niccolò laughed. Essentially, he said, it didn't matter what I liked or didn't. What mattered was making the system work to one's advantage. And we happened to be living in a system where people put their titles on their doorbells. Italy, he explained, has always been a class-based society. There is power in certain professions. Titles make one's stocks rise. Professional school qualifications, like accountant and surveyor, will work too. But *dottore* or *dottoressa* are best.

I frowned. 'In English, 'doctor' is used only for medical experts wearing lab coats.'

He smiled. 'If you don't believe me try it and see. Think of it as a cultural experiment.'

I spent the week that followed *dottoressa*-ing left and right.

I called myself 'doctor' in every e-mail, introduction, and phone call. I said it at every bank, public office and real estate agency I visited. The results were astounding. Incredibly enough,

I was offered coffee at the Comune, called back immediately for several decent housing opportunities, and was always greeted in the formal verb tense. Like it or not, this doctor thing produced results.

When the next urgent translation appeared out of nowhere, I stopped by Nico's studio again.

'How like a secret agent you are looking today', he greeted me.

'A *secret agent*? What is that supposed to mean?'

'Professional and glamorous.'

'Kind of like a *dottoressa*?'

'Better.'

'You know, I've been dying to kick someone in the shins all week. Maybe it will be you.'

'Don't do it', he said, 'I could sue.'

They win in the end, you know. *Dottoressa* or not. They always win in the end.

Positive thinking

In Italy, a best friend is known as a 'heart friend', and my *amico del cuore* is Giorgio Moro. Although this is not top-secret information, I do have some qualms about using his full name in print. Any writer will tell you that it is inadvisable to tie a character so closely to a real person, but in Giorgio Moro's case, I can't help it. There are two reasons for this. First, as his best friend, I feel the need to differentiate him from all the other Giorgios in the world. The second reason is that we grew up together. His mother would use his first and last name whenever he was in trouble, and Giorgio Moro is still in trouble often. As kids we made a very complementary pair: he was always busy trying to get into mischief and I was always busy trying to stay out of it.

Giorgio and I were summertime neighbors in this lifetime and have agreed to be siblings in the next one. Especially if we both end up in Italy again. Around here, it's good to have your friends as part of the family.

Giorgio has *amico del cuore* status for several reasons. The first is that he loves life. Complete stranger to the melancholy neurosis that so often creeps under my own windowsill, he is the token Italian optimist. Stranger to worry and friend to all that is bold and unpretentious, Giorgio Moro has various preferred phrases that he uses to raise my spirits. His favorite is 'stop drowning in a glass of water' and my favorite is *ci penso io*.

For the untrained ear, *ci penso io* may sound like 'I'll think about it.' In reality, when Italians need time to consider an idea, they simply say *ci penso*. The two expressions appear to have the same literal meaning but they are worlds apart. That final *io* carries all the weight and is usually accompanied by a wink of complicity. It means 'you just sit tight, I'll worry about that.'

This Italian form of reassurance should be received with some measure of relief. You have a problem, but they're going to take care of it for you.

Italy is a wonderful country but it does offer its share of trivial challenges. Sometimes, when I'm not paying attention, my need for a new world order gets the better of me. In other words, I start feeling sorry for myself. *Every room in the house takes a different type of plug. My flat is a breeding ground for mosquitoes. The Signora who cleans the stairs earns more than I do. The actors who dub movies into Italian all have the wrong voices. Do I really want to be the only one in this country who declares all of her income? Should I order* tiramisù *or* gelato alla fragola?

When Giorgio interrupts my outbursts and says *ci penso io*, it means he's planning to buy me a multipurpose electrical adapter. Or he's going to introduce me to the Vape mosquito-murdering machine and find me a translation to do for a little extra cash. He's also considering asking his accountant to fill out my tax form. Or he may just take me to a film in the original language and order me the dessert he knows I really want to eat. *Ci penso io* is so very good at saving the day.

In addition to its practical value, I find the phrase among the most telltale of expressions. To me, its wording reveals one of the primary characteristics of Italian living. Thinking does not necessary lead to action but it might. Thus, *ci penso io* is a perfect expression for a country where so much of life is based on what 'might happen.'

In Italy, helpful intention undoubtedly exists, but one cannot be certain that the Fates will cooperate. That's why, around here, it is safest only to make implied promises. With *ci penso io*, you can make a promise without really making one. Should anyone accuse you later for not coming through, you've got your bases covered. After all, with *ci penso io* you only agreed to 'think.' Possible action was insinuated but not technically promised. If your efforts fail to produce results, you have a built in linguistic alibi.

All this brings me to the other main reason that Giorgio Moro is my heart-friend. He may be incorrigible and impulsive at times but he almost always keeps his promises, even the ones he only implies.

'I'm writing about you and I'm going to use your full name', I told him the other day. 'With you in the story, it only took a paragraph before I broke my first rule of storytelling.'

'I was born to make you break rules.'

'Yes. It's lucky for me, that deep down you are good.'

'*Good*?' Giorgio grinned. '*You* worry about being good. About the rest, *ci penso io*.'

Just a wish away

I spent my first years in Florence teaching parts of speech to mother-tongue English speakers who were in Florence to earn their international teaching certificate. Most of my students considered grammar the bogeyman man under the bed. Now my stints as 'grammar girl' are limited to a few English lessons a month with my businessman friend who needs to speak the language when he travels the world. Before our last lesson, Andrea, worried about his looming London trip, prepared a series of 'everyday' dialogues with the help of a computerized translator. Alas, trying to convince an elementary student of the uselessness of such devices is like trying to squeeze blood from a turnip. But it was my job to try.

'In English, we don't say "I would want a ticket, please". "Want" is not usually used in the conditional', I told him.

'Why?'

'Well, because we save the phrase would want to talk about things we wish for: if I could eat anything in the world right now, I would want a double chocolate cheesecake.'

'It means you're hungry for cake but there is none?'

'Exactly.'

Andrea thought for a moment and then smiled. 'In Italy, we always use "would want" to ask for things. *Vorrei* leaves room for the thrill of doubt. In America, you are always very sure that you can have what you want, as long as you pay for it. That is the biggest difference between our two countries.'

'Oh, no', I sighed. He had said this with an off-handed nonchalance, but a comment like that can drive me to three straight nights of cultural insomnia. My student left the lesson half an hour later happy as a clam.

With three written dialogues folded in his pocket, he'd feel safe at the airport, the hotel, and the museum ticket window. He had been trained to make reasonable requests. I watched him go with 'the thrill of doubt' whirling in my brain and the weight of *vorrei* on my mind.

The more I think about it, the more I find that requests represent the root of cultural experience. If you want to know about a country, discover how people ask for things. Why? Because the art of exchange is one of the building blocks of society. After all, communities are born once people start trading.

In Italy, all requests are wrapped in wistful longing. With *vorrei*, even ordering in a restaurant is cause for suspense. You are welcome to say *vorrei una bistecca ben cotta*, but if you're in Florence, the chances of the waiter actually fulfilling your yearnings for a well-cooked steak are about as likely as winning the lottery without a ticket.

The use of the conditional here is very apropos. You can want all you want, baby, but you ain't gonna get. Steak has to be eaten rare. In Tuscany, a well-cooked T-bone is not considered a legitimate craving. For Italians, the success of requests always depends on the validity of the desire.

In efforts to soften their sense of entitlement, English-speakers also use the conditional for making requests, but their slant is entirely different. In English, we place all our eggs in the 'customer service basket.' Only people who truly believe that clerks are there to please the customer could invent a phrase like 'I'd like a ticket to Bristol, please.'

In Italy, a passenger who tells the conductor *mi piacerebbe un biglietto per Brindisi*, will more likely get a smirk than a ticket. But then, the same would probably occur in Britain if a nervous man in a bowler hat came rapping on the Plexiglas with 'Sir, I would be immensely pleased by a train ticket, thank you.' *Vorrei*, the key word for conditional desire, is much more likely to get you what you need. But 'the thrill of doubt' always applies. In the art of Italian exchange, a clerk's job is not to keep the customer satisfied: it's to judge whether or not the client can or should be made happy.

The essence of *vorrei* hit home for me after my last move. I called the telephone company and had a lengthy conversation with Paola, Wind telephone operator number 3456. I had dialed the toll-free number with high hopes. In the age of mass communication, the possibility of a home phone did not initially strike me as an unreasonable appeal. '*Vorrei l'ADSL ed una linea telefonica*', I told the Wind lady.

'I'll have to see if you are allowed one', she answered.

It took only a 10-minute check to prove that I was somehow worthy. 'Okay', she said. 'I've put you on the waiting list.'

'Waiting list? But how long will it take to get the line activated?'

'Minimum 45 days. Maximum 180.'

'But 180 days is six months!' I protested.

'Yes, but that's the maximum wait.'

Not that I want to be cynical, but in Italy, one shouldn't even bother to remember the minimums. The maximum wait always applies. I argued with the woman for another 15 minutes and then hung up. Paola would not listen to reason. Hysteria did not inspire her to take immediate action against third world telecommunication policies.

Resigned, I signed up for the waiting list. Forty days or 180. The 'thrill of doubt' did almost nothing to curb the stinging inevitably of six months without an Internet connection. There's always a bright side, though. Paola's inability to do 'what I'd like' helped prove my newest linguistic theory. In Italy, purposeful requests almost always turn into pining. *Vorrei* does its job beautifully. 'I'd want a phone line—if I could have anything in the whole wide world.'

As it should be

Italy is a country where food must always be served at the right time and temperature. Thus I find Sunday brunch the easiest way to entertain. I say this for two simple reasons. First, I am a morning person who makes a mean pancake. Second, the prospect of serving pasta to *al dente*-obsessed Italian guests scares the living daylights out of me. Thirty misplaced seconds of boiling time decides whether or not your friends will go away hungry. And I just can't take that kind pressure.

A few Italian friends came for brunch last weekend. As we waited for the teapot to whistle and the coffee to 'come up', my guests engaged in a spontaneous round of beverage-based trivia. *To get a coffee* come si deve *you have to go to Naples: the water is somehow special there and it makes all the difference.*

To drink tea come si deve *you have to give the pot a teabag of its own. To get a cappuccino* come si deve, *you must avoid re-heating the milk. Otherwise, the fat evaporates and the foam becomes pure air.* I listened carefully to the canons of properly fixing breakfast drinks and no one caught my fugitive smile. Italians are a rather flexible people, but mealtimes somehow propel all their non-negotiable expectations to the surface. The phrase *come si deve* or 'as things must be' suddenly sprouts out of nowhere, the way mushrooms come up after a rain. In truth, the only safe way to feed Florentines is to fix something they have no idea how to make. Otherwise, you'll tempt your guests to spend the entire meal telling you how things were *supposed* to taste.

It took me at least five years to master this principle and double that time to understand that this Italian brand of boldness is not meant to offend the cook. Still—one must be brave when cooking for Italians. Try as you might, there will always be something to correct. In this country, the table is common ground for comment and though your final product may taste good, it still could have been prepared 'badly.' When it comes to cuisine, the end does not always justify the means.

To Italian taste buds, the art of cooking is like playing a good game of cards. To win you must know where the face cards stand in relationship to each other. If the ace takes the king and the lady takes the jack, then you must play that way. Peas take parsley. Mashed potatoes take nutmeg. Spinach takes garlic. Those are the rules. Changing the condiment constitutes cheating. So, to make fried meats *come si deve* you must use sage. Proper rump roast calls for rosemary. Tomatoes will always take basil and *nipitella* goes with *funghi*. The fact that you've never even heard of *nipitella* is of relevance to no one; you should have used it to season your mushrooms nonetheless.

Come si deve does not just apply to food, of course. To be a *dottore come si deve* you must really listen to your patient's heart. To be a hairdresser *come si deve* you must look at the shape of your client's face before you cut her hair. To be a politician *come si deve*, you have to stop practicing politics. The phrase 'as one must be' testifies to personal excellence and moral soundness.

I love to see it used for food. After all, food *is* a moral issue in Italy. But the rigid sense of expectation with which Italians await their plates is only partly a question of the palate. Italy is a dynamic country, where rules change with astounding frequency. Laws are written, approved and then quickly re-drafted to suggest the exact opposite. Two-lane roads toss in their sleep and turn one-way overnight. Alley-ways get their names changed and no one warns the neighbors. If you live in a world where obstacles can be found everywhere but on the restaurant menu, it's comforting to know that food can be trusted to taste as it should.

English speakers may combat chaos by keeping single file lines and choosing street names that follow the order of the alphabet. Italians gratify their sense of order by making sure their herbs are in all the right places.

When I turned my attention back to my friends and their brunch-time debate, Filippo was bragging about his intimidating visit to the breakfast cereal aisle in an American grocery store. At the time, he'd felt panicked by the overwhelming amount of choices. In retrospect, he was impressed. 'In Italy we have only three cereals and still manage to lead fulfilling lives. I don't know how we do it', he said, reaching over to squeeze my shoulder.

'For cereal *come si deve*, you have to pour cold milk on top and eat it while it's still crunchy', I told him. 'Italians pour their cornflakes into warm milk and wait for them to get soggy. You people may lead life right, but you do breakfast cereal entirely wrong.'

'So, you like your cereal *al dente*?'

'There's really no other way, baby.'

My friend and I laughed together. It was barely past mid-day and we'd somehow reached a summit of cross-cultural understanding. Some things just are the way they are. And there's nothing like the sweet comfort that comes with allowing them to be 'as they must.'

Mortal pizza

Giacomo, Simona and I were sitting on empty blue milk crates in front of Elena's pizzeria. Only the line that stretched outside her pizza-producing hole-in-the-wall provided a clue that Elena had recently been named the World Champion *Pizzaiolo*. My friends had been coming to eat there, and only there, for 10 years at least—to Italians, excellent wood-burned pizza merits an exclusive love relationship.

After half an hour of freezing outdoors, we were invited to crowd around a tiny table reserved for loyal customers. Spurred by the voracious grumbling of my stomach, I began to scrutinize the menu with real urgency. 'Get the pizza with *radicchio* and *taleggio* cheese. *È la sua morte*', Giacomo told me.

'*È la morte sua?*', I asked bewildered.

'Yes, it means "it's the best there is".'

'You say "it's its death" to mean "best"?'

'Only when you talk about the pairing of two things. Like hot chocolate and whipped cream', he explained. 'Separate they are good, but together they become truly complete—a perfect blend of flavours. That's when you use *è la morte sua*.'

I'm sure you can guess what happened next. What could I do but hound my poor friends to provide me with multiple examples of dying food-duos? Luckily, Simona has been to cooking school and was quite good at thinking up food combinations that perish thanks to perfection.

Soft cheese with pears, aged *pecorino* with honey and *gorgonzola* with walnuts. San Daniele ham and cantaloupe. Soft bread with heaping spoons of Nutella.

'So, are these personal preferences or are they universal truths?' I wanted to know.

Simona thought for a minute. 'Perfection isn't really a question of personal preference. But it's not only about mixing two foods', she continued, '*È la morte sua* can be used with any fantastic combination. Christmas with snow, *è la morte sua*.'

I shuddered. 'Sorry, but it sounds like you're saying that snow is the death of Christmas. This expression is really ugly when you translate it into English. I really can't think of anything worse than "the death of Christmas".'

'Death is perfection, Linda', Giacomo insisted.

'Not in my book.'

'Well, life certainly isn't perfect, so death is the only thing left', Simona mused.

Giacomo and I both turned to look at her. 'That's pretty profound for a Saturday night', he said with undisguised admiration. They love each other, and she, I think, is the death of him.

Thankfully, the waiter came and we ordered three *radicchio* and *taleggio* pizzas. One simply cannot argue with unopposed exquisiteness. As for the cultural significance of Simona's statement, I just didn't have the strength to elaborate. Hunger blocks all basic analysis. And besides, her wisdom pretty much speaks for itself. We lived in a country where people readily accept and expect life *not* to be perfect. Perhaps, *that* is the key to Italy's high quality of life.

For those who are wondering, dinner was scrumptious. *Radicchio* and *taleggio* is definitely a keeper. Is it the death of pizza? I don't know—but it certainly is to die for.

'Mamma mia'

My mother says that if you really hate something, the best thing to do is spend time with it. Once enough hours have passed, it will become your friend. Spend time with your enemies and you will develop empathy for them. Spend time with your detestable list of conditional verbs and you'll end up wanting to carry a copy in your wallet. Spend time with your fears and you'll develop a strange affection toward them.

I have been wanting to write about Italian mothers for more than a year. If you must know, I sit down twice a month to write an article, and more often than not, I start by declaring to the keyboard that I want to write about *la mamma*. Unfortunately, the keyboard never cares to cooperate. And it always refuses to let me write about mothers.

It's quite a titanic task, you know. There are stereotypes lurking at every corner. Each time I start on *la mamma*, the overbearing meal-maker who irons her son's socks always butts her way onto my page and won't budge an inch. Try and fight against Italian mothers, even imaginary ones, and you'll most likely lose. The only way to have my way is to outsmart her. And in this case that means I have to spend some time with the things I most fear.

Mostly, I'm frightened by two things: the stereotypical and the trivial. They are mortal enemies to the writer in me. But maybe today I can find the strength to love my enemies for an hour. Because I just have to get this over with. I have to write about mothers in Italy so I can stop thinking about them.

So brace yourselves and bear with me. Here is what I've observed about mothers in Italy: *la mamma*'s ability to make life both easy and difficult surpasses all expectations. She is paradox incarnate. No one else knows how to occupy such contrasting roles with such

poise and grace. She serves at the table but rules the world. She is stagehand and starlet. A beacon of self-sacrifice who always gets her way, *la mamma* serves like a foot soldier and commands like a general. She is martyr, warrior, servant and queen. Maybe that's why, in Italy, her word means everything. The phrase *mamma mia*, like the mother it recalls, works in all situations.

Mamma mia is 'No way!', 'Imagine that!', 'Incredible!', 'Wow!', 'No problem!', 'What a bore!', 'How exciting!' and 'What a nice surprise!' More similar to 'my God' than 'my mother', this prized piece of language covers the entire range of human experience. It conveys wonder and implies surprise; it reveals horror, shock and disbelief. It can mean dismay and disapproval. It can stand for appreciation and awe. Italian mothers cannot keep secrets. Neither can *mamma mia*. It says it all. In Italy, anything that's worthy of interest or comment has a bit of mommy in the mix.

Perhaps the most common Italian expression, *mamma mia*

is used to protest against high prices, pouring rain and rude neighbors. You can say it when a child brings you daisies. It's good for marveling over how much your nephew has grown. It's great for bemoaning the state of the universe. Like the mother it mentions, *mamma mia* can carry the weight of any emotion.

Last Friday night, I met my friends Claudia and Daniel for *bistecca* and boar sauce. Children of Italian mothers, all three of us spent the better part of our childhood in North America and then moved to Europe to live out our adult lives. They both work for the United Nations in Rome. Daniel has spent the last six months on a World Food Project mission in Afghanistan and Claudia has recently returned from an emergency training camp in a place I'm not allowed to mention. Her job was to take important diplomats hostage to see how they would react to emergency situations. In their company, my life in Florence was utterly mundane.

After an hour of world hunger, social unrest and puppet governments, I started to feel antsy. What am I doing with my life? Shouldn't I be out saving the world too? Just in time, our conversation took a fortunate turn and we started talking about our mothers. *Did yours make you eat squid* risotto *in the school cafeteria? Did yours make you wear crocheted underwear? Did yours become suddenly obsessed with your bowel moments as soon as you set foot on Italian soil?*

Admittedly, all very trivial topics. But sometimes the world is a big bad place and there is something therapeutic about talking about *la mamma*. It helps you remember where you are from. It might even help you remember where you are going. Amongst the laughter, I told my friends about my interminable mother-based writer's block.

'I'd say that *mamma mia* is a good saying for grown-ups, because deep down we are just kids busy making a mess of things',

Daniel said. He smiled but something sad was happening behind his eyes. He had seen more of the world than I'll ever care to.

'My mom used to make peanut butter sandwiches by folding the slice of bread over. It was her effort to integrate', I told him. 'Everyone else had isosceles triangles with the crusts cut off.'

He squeezed my hand and laughed, letting the mood be light again.

I went away from that dinner with a few worthy realizations. The first is that I know nothing about civil rights in Afghanistan. The last, and most important, is that adults should be encouraged to use *mamma mia* often. It's only a few words away and you never know when you'll need a bit of mother in your world.

Sweet house

There is no real word for 'home' in Italian. And although the expression *casa dolce casa* does exist, it rings like 'house sweet house' and holds none of the curl-up-on-the-couch-comfort, we project onto the expression in English. And although, I have always felt 'at home' in Italy, I've spent much time wondering why Italians have failed to invent a word as lovely as 'home.'

Casa may as well be an architectural plan and the antiquated phrase *focolare domestico* does little to convince me. Admit it: 'domestic hearth' is a bit of a stretch.

During my time as an adult in Italy, I have rented innumerable apartments, both furnished and unfurnished.

Rental laws in this country guarantee that once a tenant is safely in a flat, landlords have no power to evict—ever. Logically, most landlords act accordingly, opting for 12-month contracts where no one is obliged to offer official residence and the year's end means 'time's up.' To make a long story short, let's just say that I've searched for myriad 'homes' in different areas of Italy and found the same amount of 'houses.' So, after 15 years and my last big move, I felt the sudden urgency to get to the bottom of this language truth. Why is there no word for 'home' in Italian?

The first reason may be historical. Italians seldom have the same sense of ownership people apply to their homes in the United States. If you own a place in an ancient city like Florence, your house always somehow 'belongs' to someone else. You may have gutted it out and renovated the building, but your fifteenth-century 'palace' still bears the name of guy whose noble heirs are alive, well and sitting next to you at the bar. Possession is hard to come by and its knots are almost impossible to undo.

 The sheer lack of space in *case italiane* may also stunt the development of home-sweet-hominess. Kitchens, for example, are often surprisingly narrow strips of space cut out from the living area. Rolling doors serve to block out the smell of frying and no one stays there longer than they must—unless they find a keen sense of comfort in claustrophobia. In many families 'A room of one's own' is often nothing more than the title of Virginia Woolf's book, and brothers and sisters sleep in bunks that are made quickly in the morning by mamma. Even in Italy's ever-increasing one-child households, the concept of 'one's own room' as we perceive the space in the United States, has yet to be wholly imported.

Italian children do not concoct projects for the science fair in their rooms or plaster the walls of their pre-pubescent lairs with teeny-bop posters. Though not inexistent, a children's power to reign over their room is limited. In fact, the American brand of adolescent freedom represented by sitcoms in the 1980s always filled my contemporaries with wonder. To my then-teenage Italian friends, Bill Cosby and his teeming teen brood were just one step away from science fiction. Theo Huxtable was allowed to live in a pigsty and no real mamma would ever let her boy sleep in the midst of such rubble.

Let's just say, that the great majority of 'own rooms' I've visited in Italy, both as a child and as an adult, have inevitably been characterized by a squeaky-clean 'mamma's-been-in-again' feeling. The second thing you notice about bedrooms is that Italians are inexplicably prone to hang pictures of themselves on the walls—and I mean 'of themselves by themselves.' 'Why does everyone put up photos of themselves alone', I remember asking Giorgio Moro once.

He grinned. 'It's the only place in the house we can get a little privacy.'

Another reason for the absence of 'home' may be the common lack of personal 'I-own-the-place' paraphernalia. Although Italian houses are not entirely devoid of knickknacks and table-top décor, the utter absence of clutter never fails to amaze the average Anglo visitor. In this country, houses host people, not packrats, and should be fashionable rather than frumpy. Amenities like floral throw cushions, wall-to-wall shag carpeting, snuggly quilts and tea cozies should not be expected. Dust-gathering tokens of comfort appall rather than appeal to Italians. In a word, they much prefer the inherent hygiene of cool marble floors and sleek, bleak furniture that Americans reserve for five-star hotel lobbies rather than homes.

But now that I've reasoned my way through house, home and *casa*, I need to tell you a story that has nothing at all to do with reason.

In my 29th year, I moved from Mantova, a provincial, but beautiful town in Lombardy where I had taught for the better part of three years. Suddenly, and without so much as a 'sorry', the school I worked for decided to cut its English courses. After a month and a half of worried unemployment, I searched my sofa for lost change. Once the apartment was sufficiently scoured, I called my cousin Carlotta in Venice. 'I'm thinking of moving again. Can I stay with you all while I look for work?'

'Don't forget to bring your water-bus pass', she said. Carlotta's response assured me that I had made the right phone call—when one is on the verge of existential and economic crisis, you've just got to search out the practical people.

I packed one red suitcase and left the rest of my things in storage. And then I took the train. Dinner at my aunt and uncle's that first night was a bit hard on all of us. I felt like Pollyanna showing up on Aunt Polly's doorstep in scuffed shoes, donated from a Ladies' Aid Convention. And I was in no mood to play the 'Glad game.'

Everyone was uncommonly quiet, and the air carried that strange brand of awkwardness that comes when you're a bit scared as to where conversation will turn.

As my aunt served up the season's first mandarins, I broke the uncanny silence.

'Well, I'm almost 30, unemployed and completely broke.'

'It could be worse', my uncle Bepi said. 'You could have not come.'

Home. Italians may not have a word for it, but trust me—they certainly get the idea.

New Year's revelation

It was only the third day of the New Year and I had already decided that I was not going to write a single word until the end of the next century. Words were my business, but paychecks never really compensate that brand of pain known as creativity. When I am struck by that particular form of self-pity known as 'writer's block', I seek out the people I knew long before I actually had anything to say. Sara, Francesco and I had met years back at a school in Mantova and had found each other in Florence again five years ago. We had inadvertently become neighbors in November—another lucky coincidence which supports the idea that one should always keep old friends nearby. I sometimes stop at their house for tea on my way home from work, especially when the day is cold and I need to be reassured that there is still warmth in this world. Only Francesco was home when I arrived that night, and since he was already drinking tea, I sank into the sofa and told him my news. 'I cannot think of a single thing to say. I'm done writing about Italians.'

'Good goal for the new year', he smiled.

His response was so mild that I decided to try something more drastic. 'Maybe I'll shave my head and move to Singapore.'

'Why Singapore?'

'I don't know—that's why I want to go there. I already know about Italy. *Basta*, I'm bored.'

'Alright. But before you go, come look at my new book.'

Francesco is a rock singer who works in a bank. If Italians had middle names, his would be Versatility. He is the only person I know who collects reference books for fun. *1001 Books You Must Read Before You Die* is his latest intimidating addition to a shelf that already holds titles like *100 Ideal Albums for Understanding the New Italian Song*, *The Ultimate Encyclopedia of Cinema* and other tomes that leave you feeling as smart as a glowworm.

I leafed through the volume of 'musts' starting with the twentieth-century section. The pitifully short list of novels I've managed to read over the years left me wondering what I have been doing with my time. 'Francesco, reading this makes me feel like an ignorant lout', I frowned.

He smiled. 'I suppose that's the feeling I was aiming for.'

'Why?'

'Because once you start feeling like you haven't already thought of everything, it means you'll be ready to write again.'

I looked at my friend. He raised his eyebrows and it was a dare.

'How did *you* get so smart?', I asked.

He shrugged. 'From watching television, probably.'

'Hmm. Do you have an "Ultimate TV Show" book?'

'No, but we can make our own list *dei più belli*', he grinned, already reaching for paper.

Francesco's eagerness to create a 'most beautiful' list made me smile. In many countries beauty is seen as food for the soul, but nowhere more than Italy is beauty the daily bread of the common man. And it's not enough to just see it, you have to talk about it as well and delight in rolling the word around in your mouth, as if it were toffee. *Bello*—the ubiquitous king of Italian adjectives is the end all be all of descriptive fervor. Before Italians decide how to deal with a person, place or thing, they verify the presence of beauty or ascertain its absence. It is the initial stage of all contemplation. In Italy, all things must pass the *bello* test. More than an aesthetic judgment, *bello* is a way to assign intrinsic worth.

Making a 'most beautiful list' with an Italian is no easy feat. Possibly the most commonly used word in the Italian language, *bello* is much harder to use than you might think. Its English equivalent is twofold and falls somewhere between the categories of 'good' and 'nice.' Much more neutral than 'beautiful', *bello* is attributed only to that which merits universal admiration. If you call something 'beautiful' in English, you're truly taking a personal stance about it. To Italians, beauty is not only a physical characteristic; it is a moral obligation and the pillar of civilization. In this country, *bello* is the starting point and not the summit—an expectation rather than a real achievement.

If you really want the scales of opinion to tip, then you have to throw your hat over the fence and borrow adaptations of *bello*. The affectionate, pat-you-on-the-head word *bellino*, for example, leaves room for doubt. It means you like something but are willing to fathom that someone else might not. Diminutive in every way, *bellino* is most commonly saved for the pleasantly cute or arguably entertaining. Contrarily, *bello*'s superlative *bellissimo* leaves no space for debate, but it does mean you want to keep talking about whatever you happen to be praising.

Our three-pronged list grew fat quickly, and an hour later, when Sara joined us, we'd already started a list of the *più belle* songs of all time.

'Sara, would you consider "My Way" *bellina, bella* or *bellissima?*', Francesco asked before she even got her coat off.

'Frank Sinatra is all three', she said without skipping a beat.

I smiled. How I loved my friends. They too, were all three.

I left feeling much better. Vanilla bean tea, The Voice and heavy books do much to heal the tired soul. Singapore was just a passing fancy. It was the third day of the year, and life was full of beautiful things. Unarguably.

Portrait of a lady

Today I'm waging another battle against a blank page and an enemy expression that has yet to reveal itself. It is Saturday and, gratefully, the press office is quiet. Most of the theatre troupe that makes the newspaper has all trooped home to weekend stage-plays. The death of my home computer has compelled me to stay here to write my column in hard-earned silence. But, despite logistic difficulties, I'm feeling optimistic: Santo Spirito is always a good corner for creating things.

As I sit in front of my computer, my colleague, Elleci, stands at the foot of his half-finished canvas. He paints on Saturday mornings and has been working on a portrait since long before I arrived. By the sound his brush behind me, he is busy winning his own artistic war against Sophia Loren's face. Or maybe it is love, not war, that he is battling against on his side of the room.

At half past twelve, we stop our weekend art endeavors and walk to Lola's for lunch, along with the rest of the neighborhood rabble. She's serving up *braciole fritte* with fried potatoes and artichoke hearts, as if she'd coined the phrase 'comfort food.' Fried steak is what she makes for us motherless cubs every weekend, to celebrate the coming of Sunday.

Today, as I squeeze into my Saturday bench-spot between the blacksmith and the frame-maker, I wonder as usual what good I've unwittingly done over the last six days to deserve such lunch-time love. Other unworthy but happy souls feel the same way, and Saturday is the day that Lola gets kissed. Hungry men turn back into boys as they step over the threshold of Lola's too-small kitchen to thank her for her trouble. I love to watch the love scenes. These men are twice her size, but she seems bigger than they. That's how it is with professional mothers who cook for a living.

Lola is both cook and waitress and serves her crowds with the curt affection of one who has too many mouths to feed. Lola's brand of love is Italy's truest form of affection. In this country, perhaps more than elsewhere, the purest sense of devotion is food-related commitment. There's no greater affection than the kind that worries over empty stomachs. To let your children, borrowed or otherwise, face life with empty pockets is possible. To send them into the world with unfilled bellies, however, is nothing short of unforgivable.

Unsurprisingly, she calls the men who eat at her tables *amore*. *Amore* is for the men only, because in Italy ladies are prone to love their boys best. Lola greets her women with the diminutive *signorina bella*. Beauty is the best way to care about girls. Whether you are technically a *signora* makes no difference. Married or not, Lola calls every lady by her single woman's title. In her mini-trattoria, we are all young maidens waiting to blossom. I suppose it's easy to see people as little if your heart is big.

After lunch, Elleci and I walk back to the pressroom 'full as eggs.' 'Lola makes art on Saturdays too', he tells me. 'Like us.'

'Yes, but her *braciole* are worth about five of my articles.'

'Maybe', he grins. 'But that just depends on how hungry you are.'

Once in the office again, Elleci quickly rediscovers his incurable infatuation with Sophia. Totally engrossed, he holds his breath as he paints, loving up a lady who is 70 and just got a calendar contract. And yet, I can't help thinking that my own 70-year-old muse is much more beautiful. She passes her months without need of a pose and she feeds the hungry. Lola doles out love in the least pretentious and most Italian of ways and serves her fans like much-loved children.

I turn and watch Elleci paint a while. There is no uncertainty in him. He knows the woman he is searching for.

And *la Loren* does have her charm, there's no arguing that. Sophia represents the Italian ideal when it comes to beautiful women. But Lola—Lola is the real *signorina bella*.

Friendly with the Fates

During my Venetian years, I lived in a crumbling, sixteenth-century apartment whose best 'room' was the terrace on the top floor. I was up there one afternoon mopping—something I did on rare occasions for the sole purpose of keeping my neighbor lady happy. She and I had developed a very friendly stairwell relationship ever since the day I carried her rubbish sacks four flights down the stairs. Be kind to your neighbor in any country, and the courtesy will come back tenfold. According to her birth year, Anna was pushing 70, but she was younger than me in every other way. Her energy was astounding and her enthusiasm contagious. And she never failed to surprise me.

As I was finishing my chore that day, Anna stepped out onto the terrace, carrying an open box with a bedraggled kitten inside. 'For you', she said simply.

Fumbling with my mop, I reached out and took the kitten in silence, with a mounting sense of alarm. It was not the first time Anna had brought me a gift. During every *tre per due* sale at the supermarket, the third of the 'buy-two-get-three' box of Barilla was mine. She'd even given me clothes from the market on occasion, saying that the vender had 'thrown them at her' as she passed his stand. But she had never brought anything as big as a kitten before.

'I'm not so sure I want a cat, Anna.'

'But a girl was taking her to *l'Isola dei Gatti* to be poisoned. And I know you're lonely, so I couldn't help but *prendere la palla al balzo*, catch the ball at the bounce. I had to take her; she is a good opportunity for you.'

The terrace was in order, but I was suddenly in an utter state of disarray. What was this about Cat Island?

Did such a place actually exist? Did people actually abandon their felines to a desolate strip of land in the lagoon and let them be murdered by someone evil who plants cat poison in the soil? Could it be true? Second, I had never made mention of being 'lonely.' Third, I am a dog person. I would not, even on my best day, call a cat 'an opportunity.'

In mild response to my series of protests, Anna said, 'In Italy, one cannot resist the will of the Fates.'

'But I'm not ready to make such a spontaneous decision', I stammered.

'This is about catching an opportunity that flies by. It has nothing to do with spontaneity. We Italians know very little of that.'

'What?', I cried. I know it was not the right time for cultural insight, but her statement surprised me even more than the cat.

Leave it to Anna to destroy my favorite myth in the time it took for the floor to dry. 'Italians are known throughout the world for their spontaneity!'

'Italians are spontaneous in their emotions but not in their choices', she informed me. Then she took the cat in her arms and told me more. 'Italy is a country of savers and slipper-wearers', she said. In this country, people choose security over spontaneity, every day of the week. Hadn't I ever noticed how small Italian fields of freedom are? Here, more than elsewhere, private adventure is often smothered by an all-encompassing sense of family responsibility. Spur-of-the-moment decisions are stifled by meals that need to be made, children who need to be raised, and ageing aunts who've got to be cared for.

There are plants to water should there be sun and shutters to close in case of rain. Bread needs to be bought before closing time and pasta can be eaten only *al dente*. A misplaced minute may spark starvation; there's no time to get distracted by futile whims—unless of course the whim is willed by what the Fates desire.

'Our belief in happy coincidence is total', Anna told me. 'That's what saves us. We are good at recognizing opportunity and *sappiamo prendere la palla al balzo*, we know how to catch the ball on the bounce.'

Hmmm. Anna and I were from different generations and different worlds. For English speakers, Opportunity is a rather timid chap. When he knocks, listen close and open up. He might not call again. In Italy, Opportunity doesn't loiter patiently at thresholds—he bounces straight through them. And there's no keeping the rascal out. He knows no locks and sees no doors. To the Italian mind, if a 'ball' gets thrown your way, you'd be a fool not to reach out and *prendere la palla al balzo*. Fear of foolishness is key. It wins the battle against the mundane.

After all, foolishness breeds shame, and sidestepping that is the Italian's primordial responsibility.

Of course, all you cat lovers out there care nothing whatsoever about all this jazz. You just want to know if I kept Snowball. So, yes, I did keep her. As Anna said, there was no way to refuse. The *palla* had been thrown, and at the time, it would have been cruel—not foolish—to let it fall.

Snowball did end up being great company, though—too great, in fact. Two years and 12 kittens later, I decided it was time to take urgent provisions. I really am a dog person, and as such, I find it quite unnerving to have a momma cat give multiple births under my bed. And despite the affection it proves, I have no patience for bats and lizards as tokens of loyalty. It was time to throw a ball of my own. I was moving to Florence and a couple cat-loving friends were buying a house in the countryside. We all agreed to *prendere la palla al balzo* and let Snowball meet her own new fields of freedom. She would go with them.

Sometimes I miss her. But mostly, I miss my young-old neighbor lady whose greatest gift to me was a couple of words strung together in a nice, tight phrase. *Prendere la palla al balzo* is never bad advice. After all, the world is round, and coincidently, it was an Italian who discovered that. Anna was a wise woman. She knew. When the world flies your way, you have to reach out and catch it.

Less bad

My friend Maureen and I were having lunch in the center of Florence. It was our good-bye lunch so I was sad and she was nervous. In a few days she was flying back to the United States to earn her PhD.

The university had provided her with a checklist of all the documents she needed for the application process. As we waited for our *pappa al pomodoro*, she waved the paper in my face. 'See', she said, 'In the U.S., if you want to do something, they give you a list that tells you how to do it. You follow the list and things work out. That's the main difference between here and there. Italy provides no check lists. You're left with just blind luck to lead you. That's why in Italy you can be happy, but you can't do what you want.'

'You mean you can't do what you plan?'

'Right. That, too.'

'So have you bought your super-duper-plan-your-life-down-to-the-last-square-organizer yet?', I teased.

'Just as soon as I step off the plane, sweetheart.'

'*Dio mio*', I said. Only God could give me comfort at that thought. It filled me with the same sense of dread I feel watching my study-abroad students charting out their days with quasi-religious fervor. Their goal is to accomplish everything on their three-month-long 'Florentine to-do list.' Of course, along with dread, I am also always invariably impressed. After 15 years in Italy, the newly arrived drive to 'get things done' fills me with a spiritual sense of awe.

Those students know where they want to go and have a little book that tells them what it takes to get them there. 'It's a mind-set', one student told me one day, almost apologetically. The houses they'll buy and the children they'll bear are all neatly squeezed into age-appropriate squares in their psyche. Life is an agenda to fill, and Americans plan their personal events with what Italians would consider shocking certainty.

Italians are different that way. It's not that they don't like the idea of future certainties; on the contrary, they are entirely enamored by them. For an Italian, a safe job, nice furniture and a windowsill from which to watch the geraniums grow–this is just a few steps short of paradise. But Italian young people tend to subscribe to subdued future intentions, rather than invest in optimistic objectives. Their life goals are too often tainted by the feasible, the probable and the likely. They *may* have a house, if their great aunt dies in time for them to be married. They *may* get a good job, if their uncle Bruno cashes in on all the favors he has coming. They may have children, if they graduate while they're still young—because everyone knows that passing the private law exam at university is nothing short of a miracle.

But speaking of law exams, I turned back to my friend. 'So when do you start?'

'I have two weeks to get settled before classes start. I really need the time, so *meno male*.'

I smiled. Like most expats, Maureen has the habit of using both Italian and English at the same time. Some ideas that are so well explained in Italian don't have a counterpart in English and vice versa. *Meno male* is one of those expressions. Translated literally as 'less bad', its English equivalent is 'thank goodness.' While both imply a sigh of relief, their starting points lie on entirely opposite sides of the psychological spectrum.

Generally speaking, English-speakers nurture a soft spot for straightforward things like goodness. The belief behind 'thank goodness' is that good will eventually prevail. If things go according to schedule or the day unfolds even better than planned, then goodness gets all the gratitude. After all, what—besides goodness—could be responsible for making the day obey one's vision of how the world should work?

Italians, on the other hand, know nothing of such sure-faced optimism and consider themselves fortunate when the 'less' fearsome option is somehow mercifully bestowed upon them.

But they never thank goodness. In fact, Italians often react to a lucky turn of events by scoffing at what could have gone *wrong* rather than singing the praises of what went *right*.

Often confused with 'it could have been worse', *meno male* differs from that phrase by virtue of its use rather than its content. In English, we say 'it could have been worse' when things really could have been worse. *Meno male*, on the other hand, means that things have turned out quite beautifully. Italians prefer personal drama to personal control and are quite content when the world presents them with a platter of 'less bad' scenarios.

Three weeks have passed since my friend hopped on her jet plane and left. That's how it is in a world where one gets to choose where to live. I am infinitely sad to see her go; her friendship was a gift to me. And I've been thinking a lot about what she said during our good-bye lunch. *In Italy you can be happy, but you can't do what you want.* Things will not work as you plan, but they will work—and often in the 'less bad' way. Italy seldom provides a checklist, but one can be happy here. One can be happy here. Thank goodness.

Playing dinner games

I must have a rare language disease. My symptoms most often show themselves at fancy dinner parties where everyone is wearing black. Somehow, understated elegance brings out all of my quirky linguistic hang-ups. At the very first lull in conversation, I find myself proposing language games and organizing people into teams based on the colors of their drinks.

I drink *Crodino*, red ginger ale, and usually lead the red team. Italians are generally not big 'game people', but if they are shocked enough they will obey almost any instructions.

The night's word game changes according to my current language obsession. At my last soirée, 'fun was had' when I forced guests to speak in the passive voice for 45 minutes. Usually, the delirium doesn't need to last so long. I can worry for three weeks about an Italian grammar point and finally get it out of my system in just 15 minutes of good solid play. This month, I've been particularly preoccupied with the verb *fare*.

Fare is the Italian form of 'to make', and once you know how to conjugate it, there's almost no use studying the other verbs on your list. As far as I can see, it is the king of all Italian verbs. Sovereign in almost every scenario, the sun never sets on *fare*. It has dibs on every mortal activity. On a given day, Italians 'make a letter' rather than write it, 'make a job' rather than do it, and 'make questions' instead of asking them. Similarly, they 'make a stroll' in the piazza when it's sunny and 'make a round' in the car when it rains. Pesky verbs like 'walking' and 'driving' are seldom involved in such leisure.

Of course, it's fair to say that both Italian and English speakers use 'make' quite liberally. In both languages people make love, requests, noise and proposals. It is also common for them to make beds, hot tea and offers one can't refuse. Similarities of expression undoubtedly exist. But bear in mind that English speakers make friends while Italians are prone to *fare amicizia*, make friendship. And to 'make breakfast' in English means you are frying eggs, whereas *fare colazione* means you're eating them. Although most mornings, Italians feel aversion to anything sunny-side up, the point is that *fare* is everywhere.

Their loyalty to the verb goes beyond the call of duty. Italians 'make tricks' and English speakers only play them. Italians 'make a swim' in the sea and 'make a bath' in the tub while English speakers have or take them. Italians 'make a party', and English speakers throw one. Italians 'make a good game', and English speakers generally play one. When people *fare discussione* ('make discussion') in Italy, it means they are arguing. Women get dolled up and 'make their hair.' Men 'make their beards' when they shave. And both sexes inevitably hope that all the fuss will help them *fare bella figura* ('make a good figure') because everyone knows that in Italy, the desire to make a great impression is second only to the need to fill one's lungs with air. If, however, you are unlucky enough to *fare brutta figura*, your real friends will insist you shouldn't *fare lo stupido*. Not that there's anything wrong with stupidity for stupidity's sake. By Italian standards, only prolonged stupidity is truly worrisome, since it will eventually *fare pena*, or 'make pity.'

One day in the teacher's staff room, I asked my colleague Beatrice why Italians use *fare* so much. She teaches Italian and knows the reasons behind these things. Bea thought a minute and smiled, 'Linda, look around, Italians *like* to make things.' If she hadn't been carrying four volumes of Italian grammar, I would have hugged her. I've never known an Italian explain something in so few words before. Italians like to *make* things, and that is the end of that.

Or almost. In reality, Beatrice's comment kept me up half the night thinking about all the things Italians like to make. There are, of course, the obvious things like frescoes, cathedrals and leaning towers. Then there's the Italian facility for making things—hence their fashion, food and high-quality craftsmanship. In daily life, their fondness for *fare* makes for quick discourse, frequent compliments and sweet promises. Italians are also famous for their ability to make-do and infamous for making things work even if it means bending the rules a bit. In Italy bending the rules is never a bad idea. *Fare* is, after all, an irregular verb.

A floor on which to dance

My co-workers and I were having a meeting and I might as well have been talking to myself. A curly white wig and a gavel to pound out 'order in the court' would have been the only way to get everyone listening to the right thing at the same time. In reality, though, the issue was quite simple: we were trying to plan a company party.

'Plan' is a very big word, of course. Throwing a shindig in Italy, they tell me, is more complicated than it is anywhere else in the world. If the authorities actually grant permission, you need a stamp on everything but the toilet paper. For real fun and live entertainment, you have to pay a series of obscure 'party taxes' in favor of commercial associations whose initials stand for B.O.T.H.E.R. And in Florence, if you want more than a half of slice of *prosciutto* per person, you have to be ready to really shell out the shillings. Luckily for all of us, there is a bright side—and our bright side was sitting to my left. His name is Marco.

Marco keeps the accounts and deals with decimals, but the man has a trait I truly appreciate: he falls in love with ideas quickly and courts them with an enthusiasm that is rare in any country. And he'll always let you describe dreams in full—before he bugs you with why they won't work. As our '*magari* man' he knows how to savor the apple before even planting the seed.

Magari is a word that's so worthy, it doesn't need an article to illustrate its greatness. It's one of those expressions that could just stand alone in the middle of a page, like a mysterious piece of modern art.

Gallery-goers could very easily gaze at this lovely little word and wonder what the artist meant by putting *magari* smack in the center of her canvas. Wistful as 'if only' and exclamatory as 'don't I wish!', *magari* stretches the mind to make more room for fantasizing. It would be a great word to paint.

Slightly reminiscent of the word 'magic', it's a banner to unborn potential and the comfort food of those whose bread has yet to bake. But beware. *Magari* is versatile to the point of being reversible, and it can cover the entire spectrum of future possibility. For highly probable scenarios like 'Do you want to come over for dinner tonight?', *magari* is 'Yes, I'd love to.' For daring propositions, that have 'impossible' written on them in red, *magari* means 'nice idea—but no way.'

If you plan on living in Italy long, you'd best get used to this ambiguity. The Italian language often leaves room for interpretation, and words sway with the mood as if conversation were a sudden summer breeze.

But speaking of changing winds, this multi-purpose word can also mean 'maybe' and serve as a worthy substitute of 'perhaps.' *Magari, ci vediamo dopo* means you'll meet on the street later in the day, destiny willing. Or possibly a year will pass before your paths cross again. *Magari* is always slow to tighten the gap between what *could be* and how the day will really end up looking. In that sense, *magari* truly mirrors the country that created it.

'I'd like to have a swing band', I told the troupe as the meeting progressed.

'*Magari!*' Marco answered, instantly impressed. 'Find me two coins to pile on top of each other and I'll find you a dance floor.'

'Forget the dance floor', Giovanni interrupted. Marco gets to dream; Giovanni's in charge of waking us up. 'We'll be lucky to find a willing restaurant. Besides, we can't get a band—the only way to avoid the music tax is to have someone perform *a cappella*.'

'We can always have you sing "Total Eclipse of the Heart"', Marco suggested.

Giovanni grinned. 'Best idea I've heard all day.' The song is part of his eight-in-the-morning repertoire and it's high time he goes public with it. '*Magari*, I do need to expand my fan base.'

I smiled. My two friends are different as day and night, but when they laugh together, there is no end to their mischief. So maybe the party will actually happen. *Magari*, Marco will find us a dance floor. *Magari*, il Giova will really sing *a cappella*. Or maybe we'll just pay the party tax and go with the band. With *magari* you never know where you'll be dancing next.

'Boh'

On the morning of Italy's last presidential election results, I purposely avoided turning on the news. There was really no need. The state of this country's political future would be written on the barman's face. I would know the results by the wrinkles on Maurizio's forehead. In Italy, breakfast always reflects the state of the world.

'So who won?', I asked Maurizio as I waited for him to prepare the foam on my cappuccino.

'*Boh*. One can't know.'

'What do you mean? Didn't they count the votes?'

'They counted. It looks 50-50. *Boh*. There's a slight lead for the left.'

This affirmation led the breakfasters to start their debate. Coffee cups were set on saucers and croissants froze in mid-air. Would there be a re-count? *Boh*. How long would it take before someone found a box of uncounted votes lying under a table somewhere, like they did in America? *Boh*. How is it that 25,000 more votes gave Romano Prodi the right to 40 seats in the Chamber of Deputies? *Boh*. Would the *Senato* be at the mercy of the foreign vote? *Boh*. With such a clean split in parliament, how would the bums ever get legislation passed? *Boh*.

I stood and watched the *bohs* bounce back and forth across the bar. Italy is a country of contrasts. Long-winded multi-faceted explanations usually abound. When trying to grapple with an issue, political or otherwise, Italians most often opt for the long version of the story. But when the going gets really rough, they jump directly into the heart of the issue. The truth is, sometimes, things have no immediate explanation. And that's when *boh* comes

out to play. It takes the place of 'I don't know' for those who are forced to admit that they can't understand.

Certainly, *boh* does not make Italy's top-10 list of the most elegant expressions. But it does serve its purpose quite effectively. One tiny syllable and you give up all anyone needs to know. Besides, what could be better than an unintelligible word to talk about the unintelligible? Fond as we are of onomatopoeia, English speakers should be able to grasp this concept quite easily. We've invented 'slam', 'bang', 'gasp' and 'smash.' Wasn't there room for a word like *boh* in all that ruckus? Why were the Italians the one to patent it?

Simple. To be able to invent a word like *boh*, you have to love the inexplicable. You have to be willing to loosen your grip on good solid reasoning. And that's where the Italians win. Either by virtue or by necessity, Italians are much better at abandoning themselves to 'that which cannot be explained.' They do not resist the unknown and are virtual strangers to the common Anglo belief that behind every event there is a reasonable statistic that will wave all our worries away.

Before setting foot on Italian soil, it's very possible that most English speakers have never even considered the need for a word like *boh*. And yes, for three days of whirlwind touring, you can make do without it. But those who have packed a suitcase with clothes for several seasons soon find that *boh* is as essential to Italian living as bureaucracy, bus strikes and boutiques with big prices.

That said, one should avoid the temptation of making *boh* into a bad habit. It's smart not to go *boh*-ing the innocent bystander who asks you the fastest way to Santo Spirito church. *Boh* is best saved for the truly inexplicable. It would be wonderful always to have highly articulate responses on the tip of one's tongue. But sometimes you just don't. Sometimes nobody does, and that's when it's best to revert to baby talk. *Boh. Boh. Boh.* It's a very useful expression. After all, you can't be held responsible for something you can't explain. And if you speak like a one-year-old, maybe someone will eventually take pity on you and throw you a biscuit.

For a nonsense word, *boh* actually makes a lot of sense. That was my realization as I stood and dipped cookies into my cappuccino—something that one is generally not allowed to do in Italian bars. Maurizio was too worried to scold me for breaking bar etiquette just then. The regular on my right ordered a *spuma bionda* soft drink and bemoaned the state of the world.

Maurizio poured his sadness into a tall fizzy glass. There was nothing left to do but thoroughly enjoy their misery.

'Prodi ought to be a village vicar. You think we'll be able to stand his sermons for five years?'

'*Boh*. Better than voting for someone who should be singing cabaret on cruise ships. If Prodi is a priest then Berlusconi is a clown.'

Personally, I vote for *boh*. It's such a delightfully sudsy word, like a bubble popping in your mouth. You may be hoping for perfectly logical discourse. Alas, all it takes is a slight drop of the jaw and the illusion suddenly pops. Things like politics are meant to remain a mystery.

By any other name

I once had a scintillating conversation with a woman who assigns an animal to everyone she meets, depending on their personal traits. All it takes is three minutes of small talk for her to decide which animal you are. I play a similar game, but my in my own whims I'm always partial to fictitious characters. I currently work with four Italian men. In my mind's eye, they are the Wizard, the Scarecrow, the Tin Man and the Cowardly Lion.

'Who's who?', my colleagues wanted to know, once I confessed my habit of assigning roles to the people I love.

'You mean you can't tell?', I asked, genuinely surprised.

The split seconds it took for them to work it out reassured me that I had cast them well. The characters, they admitted, suited them. Only Antonio was unhappy. 'Why do I have to be the Cowardly Lion?', he protested.

'Because you over-react like he does, and besides, the Scarecrow and the Tin Man are already cast.'

'You're not very kind to me', Antonio said, only half resigned to the role of the temperamental King of the Forest.

'Sorry, but unlike you, I'm not a member of the Compliments Crew.'

'The Compliments Crew?'

'Yes, you people use more pet names in a morning than I use in a month.'

None of my co-workers had noticed this, of course. I, on the other hand, had been studying the phenomenon for months. *Vezzeggiativi*, easily the ugliest word in the Italian language, is how you say 'terms of endearment.' Affectionate words are tossed around our office with astounding frequency. If you are ever feeling blue, all you have to do is reach up and grab one. There are dozens

of them to be had, and they vary depending on the time of day.

Cara is my personal favorite. It shows its face at the beginning of the shift, when the morning is young and the day is yet to be written. Quite similar to 'dear', its English equivalent, *cara* is best for kind negotiation and amicable agreements. Safe and without much string attached, it is the pleasant reminder that in Italy one can be friends as well as colleagues.

Which brings me to an important point. As far as I can see, the use of a *vezzeggiativo* is not a sign of sexism in the workplace. My four colleagues shower each other with the same type verbal affection that they use to dote on female co-workers. For them sweet words just make the language lighter. In Italy, terms of endearment should be taken as a sign of high regard and respect rather than an insult or means of condescension. Why? Because they indicate you are well-liked. And in Italy, if you are well-liked you are also respected.

Bella, Italian *vezzeggiativo* par excellence, is most often used at the end of the day. After all, there is nothing smarter than sending a woman away feeling beautiful. Certainly more common and less incriminating than its English-speaking equivalent, *bella* rolls quite quickly of the tongue. More a sign of affection than an aesthetic reality, *bella* knows nothing of the high expectations held to the adjective in English. To be called 'beautiful' in the English-speaking world you have to wear a striking red dress and raspberry lipstick. To be *bella* in Italy all you have to do is show up for work.

Yes, it's lucky to live in Italy. There are so many lovely words to be had here. However, there are some *vezzeggiativi* that should be avoided at all costs. *Adorata*, for example, is one of those words. Beyond the shadow of a doubt, a declaration that starts with *adorata* ends in argument. Not that I have any philosophical problem with being adored. My aversion to the term is purely practical. Adoration is the bearer of bad news.

'*Adorata*, the deadline has been moved forward and the budget has been cut back. But surely you will find an easy solution.' When *adorata* pops up, whatever is baking is burning. So, if you happen to hear the term, either flip on your problem-solving switch or slip out the door. They may love you, but they are going to ask you to do something difficult.

There is only one term of endearment that I fear more than *adorata*. Antonio used it with me last week. It was Friday afternoon and I called the office about a fax that needed to be sent by four o'clock.

'Will you take care of it?', I asked Antonio.

'*Certo, ciccia*. Consider it done.'

Ciccia? His unfortunate *vezzeggiativo* hit me like a brick. What did Antonio mean by calling me 'chubby?' Was my Lion friend getting back at me for the 'Cowardly' comment? Or was he simply unaware of the psychological repercussions of 'chubbiness' on the modern woman's mind?

'Listen Antonio', I told him, 'Never call an English-speaker *ciccia*.'

'Why not?'

'Just don't. It translates terribly. You'll loose a friend. She'll worry about her weight all weekend and come to work on Monday moody and bitter.'

'*Ciccia* is not meant to be insulting. Chubby women have always been considered attractive. For centuries, fat was considered a symbol of abundance. But, it's not literal, Linda. It's just for affection.'

'I understand, Antonio. But of all the awful affectionate words in the world, "chubby" takes the cake.'

Antonio laughed. He has learned to humor me and my linguistic hang-ups. '*Va bene*. Have a good weekend, *bella*.'

I hung up happy. It's true, I'm sure of it. 'Beautiful' is always best for goodbyes.

If they are roses

In my harried search for worthy Italian phrases, I try my best to steer clear of proverbs. Certainly, Italian is full of tempting proverbial expressions designed to delight the ear and intrigue the listener. 'The cat that walks through lard, leaves paw-prints' and 'if it's not soup, it's wet bread' could definitely fill a rainy day's worth of wondering. But as far as I can see, proverbs come with built-in morals, and this ultimately defeats the purpose of writing about them. It's like exploring territory that has already been rented.

That said, I am suddenly free to share my favorite expression without fear of sounding too preachy-teachy. *Se son rose, fioriranno* is my exception to anti-proverb rule.

'If they are roses, they will bloom' is the most practical romantic phrase ever invented. I find it the perfect combination of idealism and realism. It speaks of flowers, growth and spring-inspired hope, but it's so rooted in reality that you'd have to be a rock to resist it. Rose bushes do not sprout avocados. Apple trees do not bare cherries come June. If you plant roses, then roses will grow.

My father and mother met in Venice's piazza San Marco. She was selling jewelry and he was buying it and both got more than they bargained for. He didn't speak Italian and she knew nothing of English, but once his purchase was wrapped, he asked her to come to coffee with him. She said no, as good girls were supposed to, and waited for him to insist like boys were meant to.

American and unversed in Italian games of 'catch-me-if-you-can', my father accepted her refusal and left the shop as quickly as he could. Rejection hurts in any language. My mother watched him go, sure he would come back the next day, to beg for a day-date, as was the custom. After all, *se son rose, fioriranno.*

My sisters and I loved their tale, and whether under the covers or around the table, we constantly begged for 'The Roses Story.' My parents always told it in English, except for the one key phase that held the tale together. *Se son rose, fioriranno.* At certain points throughout the narrative, they'd give us the lead '*Se son rose...*', and we'd simultaneously exclaim, '*fioriranno!*' As far as words go, that one's my first love.

My father, of course, did not come back to her shop the next day, despite my mother's new push-up bra and breakfast announcement that she would be late for dinner because *un bellissimo americano* was going to walk her home.

Come closing time, she wasn't worried. She opted for long way home through the tourist section of town. *Se son rose, fioriranno.*

My parents bumped into each other in the Mercerie district and his second offer for coffee got a quick 'yes.' The man was foreign and the woman was smart—despite social convention, two invitations sometimes suffice. He walked her home for four days straight and took a plane on the fifth day. They spent the next year writing and translating letters that said nothing more than the weather report. He returned for 10 days to visit and fashioned her a marriage proposal that really was a proposal, 'Will you marry me? I'll bring you back to Italy every other year.' They set the date for the following November and he was allowed in her house to make the engagement announcement.

My grandmother's reaction occurred in the bathroom—the only room in the house with a lock. 'The man could be a psychopath. We know nothing about him.'

My mother's answer was simple, 'He is of Italian descent, Catholic and has never been married before. And that's what I want.'

When they unlocked the door, my grandfather was marching around the table singing 'Viva l'America', but his wife still needed to talk to the priest. Holy ties stretch across oceans and Father Marino was asked to call Saint Teresa's in Oakland to get references from a priest who, of course, had never seen my father before in his life. The priest in California, who doesn't get a name in the story, looked up my American grandmother in the directory. When the poor woman realized a priest was calling regarding her son, she burst into tears. On her side of the world, when a Father So-and-so calls your home, it means death, not marriage.

'Your son isn't hurt.' Father So-and-so assured her, 'He's getting married, but we need references.'

My relieved grandmother was happy to oblige. The news was a surprise, but her own need for references were already taken care of. For years she'd been praying to Sant'Antonio to help my father find a good bride. Saint Anthony deals in lost things and soul mates, and a nice lady from near his home town of Padova made perfect sense. *Se son rose fioriranno.*

With holy approval, my parents appeared at Venice's city hall to apply for their wedding paperwork. When asked his profession my father declared himself a gardener. Superintendent of Grounds and Maintenance at UCSF was just too complicated a concept and his limited Italian would only allow for 'I work with gardens.' While my mother had no problems with gardens, the bureaucrat behind the desk found the prospect appalling. If you are going to marry *un bellissimo americano*, you've got to do better than hedge clippers. 'Botanist' sounded much better on paper, he insisted, and that quickly became my father's new profession. Either profession works quite nicely, when you believe in roses.

And so that's the story—or at least the beginning of it. Needless to say, several essential elements of my moral education grew from this story: when you mean 'yes', say it. When you love someone, even weather talk is exciting. Saint Anthony hears prayers. Good priests give you the benefit of the doubt. The profession does not make the man. When you make a promise, keep it. And have faith—if they are in fact roses, sooner or later, you'll see the garden grow.

'Un'americanata'

When Giorgio Moro wants to go to the movies, it means I'm in for a B-rate film whose ending inspires hara-kiri. It's not his fault, he says, Italian movies are made that way. Unhappy endings make his countrymen happy.

'I don't want to see an Italian film', I protested at his invitation. 'They kill all the main characters and you feel like you're the only one left in the world when the credits come up.'

'So what do you propose—*un'americanata*?', Giorgio demanded.

'Yes, that's exactly what I propose.'

Anything exaggerated that glitters with rootless New World optimism can be called '*un'americanata*.' Although used not only in reference to cinema, the expression often describes a blockbuster where pre-political Arnold Schwarzenegger kills 47 guerilla soldiers with a single bullet. It can also refer to an 'America saves the world' flick or an eternal-love-in-a-minute movie where amorous intentions are declared in death scenes where no dying actually happens.

'I mean it', I continued, 'I can do misery on my own, thank you very much. Take me to see something happy for once. Let's go to a romantic comedy.'

'Nothing romantic is ever comedy, Linda. And a little bit of *realismo* won't hurt you.'

'*Realismo*? Tax fraud and bus strikes are not entertainment, Giorgio. Take me to a film where everything works out in the end and where you know whose side you're supposed to be on.'

'Life is not so clear cut.'

'I'm not talking about LIFE, I'm talking about the CINEMA.'

'But Americans so often confuse the two, don't they?', Giorgio replied in the lofty voice he uses to taunt me.

'If you make me mad, I won't go.'

'Well, I'm not going to see *un'americanata*.'

'Fine.'

'Fine.'

My attempts to give Giorgio Moro the silent treatment never last more than three seconds.

'You don't like *americanate*, but *italianate* are even worse', I told him.

'What do you mean by *italianate*?', he wanted to know.

'When Italians take something totally out of context and ruin it. Like the time you mashed peanuts and butter together and told me you didn't like peanut butter.'

'I was 12 years old, Linda.'

'Yes, and you still are, darling.'

'Ouch.'

'Besides that, you're jealous.

'Jealous? Of what?'

'*Americanate*. Limousines, all-you-can-eat salad bars, three-story ice-cream cones, king-size beds and six-lane highways. Anything ostentatious.'

Giorgio Moro sized me up and doubled the stakes. 'Double-decker sandwiches, pom-pom girls in princess gowns, smiles showing 32 teeth, Christmas cards where the dog is part of the family. Pathological idealism, quasi-neurosis', he concluded.

I smiled. 'Yep. Jealousy, pure and simple. You'd die to have your picture hanging on someone's refrigerator.'

Giorgio shook his head. 'No, Italian refrigerators are too small. We don't have the space for *americanate* in this country. Big cars and wide smiles don't fit. But I'm not jealous. Americans build a replica of Venice in Las Vegas and then tell you they've been to Europe.'

'You lie.'

'No, I swear, a woman told me that once.'

'Well, it's comforting to know you're dating quality women.'

'Listen, comforting, come to the cinema with me. Come to see a depressing Italian film. I cannot face mafia, poverty and political resistance alone.'

'Alright', I sighed, 'But if the good guy dies, you're dead, Mister.'

'I'm not too worried', Giorgio Moro replied. 'It will be almost impossible for you to even decide which one's the good guy.'

'Yeah, and not just in the movies.'

'Proof that *realismo* is more than just a genre', he grinned.

'*Realismo* means you're buying the popcorn.'

'A three-liter bucket of popped corn and fake butter fat— imported *americanata* at its best!' he replied utterly satisfied.

Drat. Just when I think I've won a cultural dual, Giorgio Moro comes back with boundless energy. The man never gives himself up for beaten. That is why we are friends. That is why he's going to talk through the entire miserable movie.

Tales to tell

The summer I turned seven, my cousin taught me an Italian children's chant about a king who begged his jester to tell him a tale. 'Once upon a time there was a king who sat on his sofa and said to his servant, Tell me a story, and the servant did begin, Once upon a time there was a king who sat on his sofa and said to his servant, Tell me a story, and the servant did begin...' The rhyme repeats itself over and over until you become completely hoarse or are knocked silly by older siblings.

My fondness for this chant earned me many life-threatening protests and the certainty that if I must die one day, I'd prefer to die in the throes of a good story. The importance of story in this culture is one of the reasons I currently live in Italy.

As far as I can see, there are few countries in the world that have as deep a love for story as the Italians. You can see it in piazzas and at kitchen tables, in bank lines and behind bar counters. Family dinner on Sundays include epic tales of woe, neighborhood scoops, and fictitious memoirs. Monday morning at the bar brings play-by-play accounts and eternal soccer sagas. Friday afternoon bus strikes prompt traffic-related cliff-hangers and long-winded narratives on bankruptcy and the city bus system. During Saturday night *aperitivo*, there's always room for romantic tear-jerkers, tall-tales and various levels of inappropriate confession.

In Italy, time is worth its weight in tales, as old and young easily exchange their hours for hearty rounds of storytelling. To the Italian psyche, stories are rosebuds to gather 'while ye may.' Without them, life's landscape becomes instantly sterile. Stories are the marrow of life. 'If there is nothing to tell about a subject, then it is worse than dead', my friend Luciana says.

It can't just be by chance, then, that the expression *non c'è storia* is the Italian cue to throw in the towel. 'There is no story' means you'd best abandon ship. For Italians, as long as there is a tale to tell, there is hope. A compromise can be reached. A solution can be found. But if there is no *storia*, it means the end has come. The beast has no breath left in it. In English, we often encourage ourselves with the phrase, 'Where there is a will there is a way.' For Italians, as long as there's a story, there's also a way. *Non c'è storia* and you're sunk.

My desk-mate at work doesn't agree with a thing I say. Despite this minor detail, he is a pretty good guy. When we first started working side by side, I would constantly propose what I thought to be good ideas and Giovanni would invariably throw thunder on my parade. He'd tell me all the reasons why my idea wasn't going to work and I would consider myself rained out. This was before I knew that in this country, protests mean next to nothing.

In Italy, dissent doesn't ruin the broth, it only livens it up a bit. So I've learned to let il Giova conjure up his 10 solid reasons why my plan won't work. By reason number 11, he usually changes his mind and decides that we can probably pull it off anyway. Things work out quite nicely once Giovanni has no more fingers on which to count reasons. It's when he becomes my ally. Ah yes, he has unwittingly taught me to face negative reactions with the fearlessness of a titan. He's proof that an Italian may shoot you down from all angles but still leave room for negotiation. Why? It's an Italian talent to say 'no' and 'yes' at the same time. Only when Giovanni adopts the phrase *non c'è storia* do I know he really means 'no.' Our negotiation is nearing its end. It means I've really lost. The game is up; the story is over.

And now I'll just tell you one more thing: sadly, I now consider myself too old for children's chants and have had to search for alternative forms of entertainment.

At present, I often amuse myself by imagining how great men in history would have been different if they had been born in a different country. I'd venture, for example, that if Benjamin Franklin had been Italian, he would not have been so concerned with spending time and money wisely. I'd bet all my pennies on it; had Franklin's wisdom met Italian ways, his proverbs would have taken a different turn. Surely, *non c'è storia* would have had considerable influence on his axioms.

Dost thou love life? Then do not squander stories, my friend, for they are the stuff that life is made of.

'Mah'

I have never been on a speed-date in my life, and I'm hoping to be able to say that until the day I die. Repeated introductions, timers and frantic checklists make me nervous. I'm just not good at having to be interesting at high speeds. Besides, when you live in a country where getting sized up is the order of the day, there's no need to torture oneself voluntarily-at least in public.

I much prefer to have my 'speed-date' sessions in private-and most of these are purely language related. Finding a nice free phrase to spend quality time with is quite a feat, especially if you're prone to weeding words out of your mind with the zeal of a gardener gone manic. This week, for instance, I've had several impressive close encounters with numerous Italian expressions. Alas, none of them made it past our seven-minute round of 'getting to know you.'

Admittedly, I am picky. A single writer seeking depth cannot just go falling in love with every word-suitor who offers her a plate at the picnic. For me, language is a love relationship, and if my heart isn't in it or I can't get my head around it, then there's just no sense leading a poor word on. Aloneness is better than bad company, and survival can sometimes depend on a very good goodbye.

When I am truly lonely for a good word to write about, I call my mother. If you want to find some truth, you've got to go to someone you can't lie to. Plus, she is a writer too, who knows better than to provide me with mere vocabulary. 'Okay', she told me over the phone last night, 'Tell me what you've learned this week.'

'*Mah, non ho imparato niente*, I haven't learned anything.'

'So, write about not learning anything.'

I refused the idea at first, of course. Partly because I couldn't see

the fun of it, and mostly because that's what you do when you're on an all-encompassing refusal rampage. But then it hit me—the word for that strange sense of inconformity I'd been carrying around with me for days. It's what Italians say, when they can't think of anything to say. It's *mah*.

Often heard and frequently misunderstood, *mah* is a complex exclamation with a myriad of meanings. Useful in times of unveiled mystery, *mah* is also known to English-speakers as 'who knows' or 'I haven't got a clue.' It's quite a bit stronger than *boh*, the other syllable Italians use to admit ignorance. Both words show that you have no idea what the final verdict will be, but *mah*, carries more skepticism. '*Mah*! That case will need a decade just to knock down the courtroom door. And once it's in, there's no telling what the judge's gavel is going to hit.'

Sometimes used to introduce discussion or resume debate, *mah* can also be a net that captures stray thoughts. It's the time you take before you jump and your chance to consider how cold the water is. Like the English word 'well', it gives you a chance to round up your run-wild ideas. *Mah*, however, holds none of the between-the-lines optimism of 'well.' Think of it as a disclaimer disguised as an extra breath. As the prelude to a thought you've never before formulated, *mah* is a buffer against false hopes. It serves to warn the world that your speedy new theory might not make it through the test drive. '*Mah*! I don't know if this will work, but I'm willing to give it a shot.'

A breath-based extension of *ma*, the Italian word for 'but', *mah* carries many of the same undertones. To the English speaker, 'but' can be one scary bugger. With a tip of its hat, it topples the tower you carefully built in the first clause. 'I appreciate your efforts, but the answer is no.' *Mah* is 'but' without the padding, and it can stand alone if accompanied by an exclamation point. The seed of doubt and the champion of inconformity, *mah* means 'I disagree.'

The reasons why are considered obvious and often left unexplained.

With *mah*, looters like uncertainty, skepticism, ignorance and doubt become the crowded inmates of a cell that's only three letters wide. In this sense, you've got to hand it to Italians. They have a knack for creating words with ant-like strength that can carry 10 times their body weight. Constantly pressed for space, Italians have learned how to pack a whole lot of meaning into a single unassuming syllable. So, while *mah* may not be a word for the highly dignified, it is both a crutch and a walking stick that can certainly prove useful for the likes of you and me.

One day, perhaps, we shall be wiser. In the meantime, it can't hurt to have a word for all the things that are hard to get your heart in or your head around. Carry *mah* with you at all times. We can never know when the hemming, hawing, stalling side of ourselves will turn up and demand dinner. We'll never know when our wild inner child will want to break out and make nonconformist angels in the snow.

For your eyes only

Italy's normally salty prices get torn to shreds when sales season comes. From *prezzi salati* to *prezzi stracciati*, when prices are shredded, it's time to go shopping. The country waits on bated breath as the stores mark down and the people line up. It was a Saturday afternoon in February and I was standing transfixed in front of a store by the station. Shopping wimp that I am, normally, I would not have had the guts to go in. Italian shop ladies have all taken a course on how to be intimidating.

The problem was they had hung my skirt in the window. I don't mean I owned it; I mean it was made for me. Knee-length, black taffeta with a wide bow on the side, I felt an immediate cosmic connection to the skirt even if I had nowhere on the planet to wear it. 'Do you think I could do housework in it?', I asked my friend Claudia. 'Or maybe just having it in my closet would be enough.'

Sighing, my friend pushed me over the shop's threshold. Claudia has no patience for platonic relationships with clothes. 'Just buy it, Linda', she told me. 'It's 50 percent off. On sale, it's almost affordable. You have to take advantage of sales' season. Normally, that skirt would cost you *un occhio della testa*, an eye from your head.'

I squinted at the thought. In Italy, beware. Expensive things cause partial blindness. In a visual society like this one, *un occhio della testa* is a sacrifice worth thinking twice about.

Claudia scouted out the racks with the eyes of a pro while I weighed the worth of my retinas. It could just be me, but I'm convinced you can tell a lot about a culture by the way it talks about money. After all, money may not make the world go round, but it certainly coaxes people to turn corners quickly. Find out how a country talks about cash and you will discover its system of values.

In English, over-priced products cost 'an arm and a leg.' English-speakers place value on the extremities; arms that reach for things and legs that reach for places. Interestingly, true worth is placed on the things we need to get us somewhere and grab us something once we get there. In the forward-moving, goal-reaching, English-speaking world, it's only natural that monetary worth adds up to appendages.

In Italy, however, the highest value is placed on the eye. This fact, in and of itself, should surprise no one. It is well-known that Italians are virtually addicted to the visual arts and arguably obsessed with aesthetic beauty. Life in Italy is not a constant chain of events; it is a constant flow of eye-based experiences. Casual visitors to this country, prove this point easily.

Their gaze fills with the beauty of Italy's palaces, paintings, and people, and they roam the streets with what look like newly-opened eyes.

Even the most veteran ex-patriots will readily admit that living in Italy implies continual bombardment for all the senses, particularly the eye. In this country, seeing is not only believing, it's synonymous with breathing.

While I was busy weighing the cultural ramifications of bodily sacrifice and monetary value, Claudia had asked the saleslady to take my skirt off the mannequin.

Had I been paying more attention, I would have tried to stop her. A naked mannequin means you're going to buy whatever she used to be wearing. 'All things considered, it's cheap!' my friend reassured me.

Never go shopping with an Italian during sales' season. You will come home with clothes you love blindly but cannot wear. Freed from the shopping spree, taffeta safely tucked in a bag with a brand name, I was struck by a feeling of elation tinged with guilt.

'Is it right to feel such a cosmic connection to clothes?', I asked my friend.

'Is there any other way to feel?', she smiled.

Right. I forgot. This is Italy.

Soccer and 'stile'

It was Sunday afternoon and we were sitting around watching soccer. Actually, we were sitting around watching people watch soccer. *Quelli che il calcio*, 'Those Who Soccer' is one of Italy's best loved programs and an absolute bore. The real matches are shown only on cable television, so my desperate group of friends were forced to watch pseudo-celebrities talk about football plays only they could see.

During the commercial break the men started talking about the World Cup championships of 2002 as if they'd happened yesterday. Traumatizing due to what Italians call 'unfair refereeing', those Mondiali were a sore spot in Italian football.

Capturing the title of 'Champions of the World' in 2006 did a thing or two to heal the wounds, but they can still get worked up about it during half-time.

I watch soccer championships with the dedication of a true fan. Don't get me wrong though, despite annual matches and afternoons of *Quelli che il calcio*, I know nothing of soccer. My interest in the subject lie solely in my conviction that national tournaments hold the secret to understanding cultural identity.

'Italians play with a grace and style that is not seen with the English and French', Giorgio Moro started in on me, 'because in Italy, *il calcio è una questione di stile*, soccer is a question of style.'

'My view of the Italian players is that they wear their hair too long and don't want to get dirty', was my biting reply.

'No. That's not it at all. It's about the philosophy of a country and its temperament. Take the Croatians and the Italians, for example. We don't get along in matches. Croatians play with the violence of their warrior past. We Italians are not aggressive on the field. For us, the game is a dance, not a war. We play better with the Mexicans.'

'Why?'

'*Lo stile* of play is similar. If both teams need a tie to pass into the next round, then the players from opposite teams help each other out and make sure no one wins.'

'You mean', I said, 'that no one on either team does a thing with the ball for the entire game to guarantee the advancing position for both?'

'Exactly, and that can only happen with people of Latin blood. We understand the value of favors', Giorgio concluded, infinitely satisfied with his verbal dissertation. 'It could have never happened with the Germans, they have a completely different *stile*.'

Watch soccer. It will tell you a lot about historical resentment and modern day political antagonism.

It will also tell you what kind of stuff a race is made of. Italians on the field go for grace, beauty, and calculated effort. They are not run-you-down, beat-you-up, leave-your-guts-on-the-field type of players.

What goes on between the goalposts, though, is a reflection of what goes on within the peninsula too. Italy is a culture where 'diving in the mud', whatever that mud may be, should be avoided even if it means compromising the game a bit. When I asked Giorgio if the way the Italians play could be a metaphor for the way they live, he turned poetic. 'Soccer, love, politics are all a game. This does not mean they are not serious. A game can be a very serious thing. You play because you believe in the game, but that doesn't mean you want to die in it.'

'Or get dirty?'

He winked. 'Death and dirt are bad for style.'

Arrangements

Writing about the word *arrangiarsi* is a bit like chasing a cricket. The little bug's been leaping all over this page with the energy of a caged pixie who knows that it's spring outside. If I don't hurry, it will hop off my computer screen, climb up to the windowsill and shimmy down the drainpipe. There are far too many people to outsmart in this world than to waste so much time with the likes of me.

This impish little word has been locked in my brain for over two weeks now, and the prime minister is entirely to blame. The morning after Mr. Prodi resigned looked like the start of a very ordinary day. I missed the bus as usual, had a cappuccino at *il solito bar* and worked a few hours in alternative bouts of banter and silence. Italy had been left leaderless, but no one had a thing to say about it.

By mid-day I could no longer stand it. Dragging my chair closer to Giovanni's desk, I begged my colleague for benefit of political enlightenment. I wanted to know more about the sudden government upheaval and the strange calm with which it had been received. Giovanni was happy to oblige. After all, he and I are desk-mates and in Italy there is no greater productive bond. Your *compagno di banco* may not be your best friend, but he can always be counted on to provide quick solutions to word problems you don't know how to answer. Italians, in general, can rarely resist the temptation of 'group-effort' and Giovanni in particular, takes his desk-mate responsibilities very seriously.

'I don't understand how the prime minister can just resign without warning', I asked. 'And why is it that nobody seems to care.'

'Oh, Prodi's resignation is just bit of healthy theatre', he told me. 'The United States is not the only place where actors become politicians.'

'But I want to know why nobody cares! The country is without a prime minister and no one's even talking about it.'

'Oh, Linda', he smiled, 'Italians *like* weak government. As long as we eat, it doesn't matter who rules us. We do fine on our own. *Sappiamo arrangiarci*, we know how to arrange ourselves. Besides, what dies today will resurrect tomorrow.'

Sure enough, Prodi slid back into his chair by the end of the week. And his countrymen gave nothing more than a nod of their heads. Centuries of invasion and tyranny have taught Italians not to pay too much heed to shifts in authority. After all, the drama of daily survival is essentially a personal one. To solve the problems of normal life, Italians do not look to leaders. To place faith in one's own smarts has always proved a smarter strategy. Thus, learning how to 'arrange oneself' is of paramount importance.

Arrangiarsi, the ability to 'arrange oneself' is all about overcoming obstacles. It flies more easily the radar than its English equivalent 'to manage things.' 'Manage' implies the scepter of command or at least the scrap of a plan. Artisans by tradition and temperament, Italians do not invest much confidence in management. 'Arrangement' is much more manual and works for craftsmen, not for kings.

Craftsmen know how to make things look beautiful, and they have transformative powers. They cannot turn stones to bread but they can make them into statues and at least feed the soul.

We may not be able to eat this dusty marble, but we'll squeeze nourishment out of it somehow. This is Italy's best-loved game. There is no bigger accomplishment than making something out of nothing. As a reflexive verb like 'wash oneself' or 'dress oneself', *arrangiarsi* captures the Italian tendency to find solutions within the intimate sphere. Unavoidable obstacles will always exist, but outsmarting The Inevitable is mostly a question of personal adaptability. To the Italian mind, even the most challenging of life's truths can look appealing if properly arranged in colorful piles.

Often called *un arte*, *arrangiarsi* also refers to being able to make it through the month without a day of official labor. The Neapolitans are said to have a special talent for it. But before we wade in the lukewarm pools of southern stereotype, note that *arrangiarsi* is a far cry from sloth.

A banner to ingenuity not laziness, it's a bold mix of intuition and uncommon instinct. It's knowing where to leap the fence. It's learning when to cry wolf and when to wear dog ears.

In the theatre of Italian life, roles and rules are secondary. Profit must know no fear and cleverness is paramount, if you're meant to survive as a mere marionette in this land of cats and foxes.

Well, that's it. Life is a nothing more than a puppet theatre, and the art of arrangement is about learning to dance without strings. But today's main character can no longer stand to stay on this page. Snappy and elf-like, *arrangiarsi* is itching to dance up some new spring storm.

Admittedly, he's not too big a fan of linguistic analysis. So let's let him out to get lost in the world. He'll make do somehow, I'm sure. His toes will show the way to green pastures even if the road is well-hidden in the woods. Maps mean nothing. *Arrangiarsi* knows how to follow his nose.

Fixed work

I have a reoccurring nightmare in which I am obliged to take a math exam for a class that I never attended. In the first part of the dream, I search in vain for the testing room. In part two, Mr. Arbuckle shakes his head at me; alas, I've failed high school algebra.

In real life, however, I love school, and that is why I always try to get hired at one. For three years, I've worked at an international fashion institute in Florence, teaching fashion-based English to 18-year-old design students. It's quite fun and luckily has nothing to do with arithmetic. But, incidentally, I couldn't make my students have nightmares about me, even if I wanted to. For these kids, someone who knows so little about fashion trends doesn't even show up on the Intimidating Radar.

Creative, talented and merciless when it came to the canons of what wears right, my students make sure I never make it through the day un-accused. The toes of my shoes are last season's shape and my hemline would be heartache for the likes of Mary Quant. I need fashion first aid, and they are more than willing to provide counsel. My own end of the bargain is twofold. I consider it my first responsibility to convince them, in English, to design an outfit that would fit something besides a Popsicle stick. The second challenge is to get them to learn the English alphabet. Before you become an internationally recognized designer, you've got to learn to spell your name for a whole lot of people.

Last Wednesday, I arrived at the institute to find the halls abuzz with a new rumor about me. 'She's not as young as she looks', someone had whispered. In Italy, anything said in a low voice is worthy of discussion, so at break students stirred my age into their coffee cups and most decided they didn't like the aftertaste. 'Good

God, she might even be in her 30s!'

In all honesty, they should have clued in much sooner. My refusal to wear sweaters with only one sleeve and my fondness for music that can still be called that are both obvious clues that I am, in fact, 'not as young as I look.'

As class started, the kids sought to set the record straight.

'Prof, are you 30?', Simone asked as people were still filing in.

I continued to erase the board with nonchalance. In teaching, suspense is everything.

'Prof, are you 30 years old?', he repeated.

I turned to face the class. 'No. I'll be 35 in December.'

I watched the lines in his forehead form as he evaluated this unfathomable truth. 'We thought you were 25.'

I couldn't help but smile. Twenty-five is the oldest they go. If you are older than them but still appear to have a reasonably active heartbeat, it means you're 25. Twenty-six-year-olds drop off their mind-screens and 30-year-olds only exist in fables. These kids understand things like mauve, Herringbone, silk and vinyl. They are geniuses with colored-pencils, and what they call doodling, I call masterful artwork. But they have no concept of practical realities or so I thought until they discovered my age.

'Nope. Thirty-five. A breath from death, you might say.'

'But if you are 35', Grazia piped up from the back, 'what are you doing working a job where you get fired and rehired again every three months? At 35, you need to get a *lavoro fisso*. You're not young anymore.'

'She's right.' Simone nodded. 'At 35, you need a pension plan.'

I have never had a nightmare on the teacher side of the classroom before. But one was suddenly well underway. 'A steady job?' Had these kids been talking to my mother? The *lavoro fisso* discussion has been banned from my dinner table for over for five years now. How could it be that my fly-by-the-seat-of-your-pants kids were suddenly acting like representatives of private pension companies?

The Italian fondness for 'fixed work' is not a new concept for me. I am well aware that for the average Italian, a contract offering work for an 'undetermined' amount of time is like being asked to sign papers promising both eternal happiness and eternal employment. *Un lavoro fisso* means you can get comfortable—the pay may be low, but benefits are great and by, law, you'll never be fired. Of course, the cost of across-the-board benefits and the perennial risk of hiring an employee who you can never get rid of, make employers weary of hiring anybody at all. Thus, being offered a fixed contract in Italy is comparable to winning the lottery. Most educated people of my generation make do with myriad temp employment scenarios.

The 'rules' of temporary labor contracts are much too detailed and purposefully confusing to be able to list here or anywhere. Suffice it to say that algebraic formulas are much friendlier. Trying to read a *contratto di collaborazione* in Italy is like listening to poor Mr. Arbuckle drone, 'If x is y and y is 2a then a is greater than b and 4b equals x.' I have signed literally hundreds of Italian employment contracts in 15 years and never know the answers to the equations they propose. Thus, I am left to nurture the slightly paranoid certainty that said math will come out in someone else's favor. It is the one area, in which I have allowed Italy to teach me cynicism.

'In truth, I'm a bit of a cynic when it comes to employment', I admitted to my class.

'No you are not', Simone said. 'You are incredibly optimistic. Anyone who works without a pension plan thinks that everything's going to be all right.'

Damn. I always knew those kids were smart. Simone's logic was bullet-proof.

I grinned at my students who were hoping we'd waste the class in prolonged chatting. 'Everything will be alright, *if* you learn your alphabet.'

They groaned. I am an incurable, fashion-less bore. And I'm old. And I am an optimist. Who would have guessed—a real live optimist.

'La privacy'

Watch how people share secrets and you'll discover the things they are trying to hide. Learn how a country exchanges confidences and you'll uncover the cornerstone of social rapport.

Italians may be known to the world as free-speaking, overly expressive individuals, but in reality, they are rather reserved when it comes to voicing their true feelings. You've got to be a bit of a detective if you want to survive in the *bel paese*.

Shy in all the ways Americans are not, Italians won't tell their intimate dreams to the lady sitting next to them on the bus. Nor do they confess in code like the Brits. In England, people discuss the price of onions and what's really being said depends on their tone of voice. In Italy, people scout out the din of unrelated chatter to disguise their tone and distract their listener. Secrets are easier to tell when they can barely be heard. Thus, in this country of narrow streets and wide piazzas, a brimming public place proves the ideal space for spilling your guts. Italians need to feel very safe to tell their secrets, and strangely enough, there is safety in numbers.

Catholic Italians, for example, practice *la privacy* in church, where the priest drones, the choir sings and all eyes are on someone else. At baptisms, communions, weddings and even funerals, family secrets find fertile ground for growing. The condensed version of break-ups, make-ups, blessings and misfortunes are swiftly passed, pan-faced, through the pews. Let's just say that most of the confessing Italians do *in chiesa* never even reaches the priest. In my family, where sacraments dot the calendar with astounding frequency, church gossip is immensely popular. There are few other places in this country where one is so effectively protected from explosive responses.

On the day my sister married, I was crowded in the second row of San Pietro Martire beside my aunt and uncle. As the wedding march sounded, zia Rina turned to her husband, 'I'm pregnant', she said.

He barely blinked and the bride made her way down the aisle. 'Couldn't you have found another time to tell me?' he whispered.

'No', she said.

In spite of myself, I nodded in agreement. The child she was carrying was number eight. Theirs was a house of *la Provvidenza* not *la privacy*. Providence reigned sovereign and privacy had been exiled for more than a decade. When you live in the clutches of mass confusion, mass is the only safe place to exchange ideas.

Of course, these days, most of Italy's families are small laic clans, who have had to find alternative spots for sowing secrets. Doorways often serve this purpose quite nicely. In the United States, people are trained to stand under thresholds in the event of an earthquake. For Italians, thresholds are the place to exchange confidences. The more earth-shattering the news, the closer they move to the door. In Italy, you can entertain your best friends from *antipasto* to *caffé* without exchanging so much as a dishful of personal disclosure. But be patient: authentic communication will arrive as soon as it's time to leave. Italian good-byes are often lingering and packed with unexpected revelations. Among innumerable attempts at *arrivederci*, classified information suddenly seeps to the surface. Job offers no one should know about yet, nameless fears that have yet to be confirmed by reliable sources and happy but unofficial surprises are exchanged in rapid passing as if one were handing off the staff of an invisible relay.

If the confession is compromising, you've already got one foot out the door and escape is easy. If the secret is begging to ride the four winds, you'll have it out in the piazza in no time. That's why thresholds are the perfect temporary portal to *la privacy*. For Italians, it's an almost uncomfortable dimension that is meant to end quickly. It's a combination of 'catch me if you can' and 'close your eyes and I'll be gone.'

La privacy does exist in the Italian dictionary, where they say it means 'intimacy' or 'reserve.' But, there is no real translation for the term, at least for how we apply it in English. For English speakers, privacy is a quasi-religious state, where aloneness becomes the key to all illuminating experience. More than *riservatezza* and less than *intimità*, privacy is the practical extension of 'personal space.' That, in fact, is the clincher: Italy is a country that generates curiosity; around here, 'personal space' may as well be 'outer-space.' Access to it is virtually nil.

But Italians are generally good sports about limited landscape and linguistic short comings. They are willing to make do with the English word and fathom the piazza a private place, makeshift though it may be.

After their first year of marriage, my sister and her husband moved to a first floor flat overlooking the corner of a piazza. If you stand in their kitchen and try to mind your own business you can still hear every word spoken in the square below. 'Aren't you ever worried that your conversations can be heard out there as well?' I asked my brother-in-law one night.

Sebastiano shrugged. 'Sound travels upwards faster than it goes downwards. That's why you should only tell secrets on your way *down* the stairs. Never on your way up.'

The Italian attention to detail will never cease to amaze me. How they manage to keep track of such things is an unsolved mystery. Otherwise, I rest my case. Italians may not have coined a word for privacy but they are certainly champions of private investigation. In this country, anything is worthy of observation. You never know what may someday serve as a worthy clue.

Pressed for pressroom

We're hunting for a new office and I've been trying all day not to write about it. But our search for a pressroom keeps sneaking into my paragraphs as if this page were the rented space the staff is looking for. So, after hours of wrestling with what I shouldn't yet share, I've decided to give in to the growing pains and tell you the story.

The people who make the newspaper have almost nothing else in common. Still, together we have that brand of fun that only dramatically diverse people can. But even fondness needs a sizeable field for growing. With three companies co-existing in an 'open space' that was originally built for the three musketeers, sooner or later, we knew we'd have to find another press room.

In Italy, however, moving is not a pick-up, pack-up event—it's a full-fledge birthing process. The first trimester of our 'move' was purely philosophical. When you work in what feels like the waiting room of an ADD doctor, it's easy to entertain the idea of a quiet corner where one can ponder the importance of commas. By month four, as the fantasy threatened to crystallize into reality, we all scrambled to find reasons to stay in the San Frediano neighborhood: *Who will feed us if we move away? Who will be our patron saint? Locked up in separate rooms, we'll all die of loneliness for sure. What an utter ode to boredom! Things are fine right here where we are,* insomma. *When all is said and done, elbow room isn't everything.*

But as nine cramped desk-spots suddenly turned to ten, it became time to come to terms with our options. We could either pump more oxygen in, or we could really move out. Thus began the practical quest to find a new tree house for the Lost Boys. Antonio and Elia dressed like private agents and went to talk to real estate

people, who showed them flats and store fronts all over Florence. With each return to the mother-ship, I hounded the harried pair with the likes of 'How did you like it?'

Most times, all I got was a shrug and a half-hearted '*insomma*.' Used in this context, it meant that the place they'd seen had too few rooms and not enough windows—or a good neighborhood, but a bad landlord, unbelievable frescos but unaffordable prices, or decent rent but poor renovation. Not too bad—but not quite the right fit, in sum.'

After months of trying to pinpoint its exact meaning, I've decided that *insomma* punctuated with a period is nothing more than a word-shield that neutralizes enquiring minds. This colorless expression tastes like tofu and is about as committal as bean-curd. Often translated as 'so-so', it saves a spot for both 'yes' and 'no' and denotes a decided lack of decisiveness.

To witness its straddling magic at work, ask an Italian any basic preference-based question.

'Did you have a good time at the party last night?'

'*Insomma.*'

Your night-owl friend either didn't particularly enjoy the soiree or he's just unwilling to admit that he was the life of the party. His real response is hidden among the two *m*'s, but with *insomma* you're being asked to do your own math. Calculate the sum any way you want—just expect the final numbers to be low.

Insomma is not known for giving gratification. The first stop on the bus to Limbo, it simply saves the speaker from having to elaborate.

No one ever really minds, of course. Italians love implied reasoning. As natural information seekers, they can usually figure things out without much help from interested parties. A tilt of your chin, a raised eyebrow, the downward curve of your mouth— Italians can easily trace the truth in every flit of your features. In this country, a clear verbal stance is often entirely secondary.

Insomma is quite a chameleon. Accompanied by a comma it's 'all in all' or 'in the end.' Give it some gumption and you've got yourself a means of impatient protest. 'Stop being ridiculous!' or 'The nerve!', it's a one-word warning to change your tune. It can also be an invitation to 'cut to the chase' because, paradoxically, the word Italians use to straddle a stance is the same one they employ to finally get a final verdict. In sum, you've reached the end of the plank. The clock in the crocodile's mouth is about to strike— so hurry and wrap up your final good-bye. Time's up. '*Insomma*! Enough already! Fly if you can, jump if you must, but for God's sake quit crowding the beam!'

Cutting to the chase, though, I'll tell you that this week, we all went to scrutinize a flat which was still completely furnished.

According to his calendar, the owner had died in May. There were still sheets on the beds and biscuits in the cabinets. Thankfully, no had the guts enough to check the wardrobes.

Insomma, *if you get over the skeletons in the closet, it's kind of a nice place.*

Will we need permission from the city to scrape off that wall paper?

All I know is that I'm painting a Brazilian landscape right above that picture of the pope.

Fine. I want my office in the laundry room.

This exchange was a good sign: no one has ever talked décor before. Lo and behold, against all prognostics, the move might actually happen—unless of course, I've jinxed it by talking about it. Oh well, let's consider it worth the risk. In this country, one can never get too attached to intentions. They are always far more mobile than people and certainly more readily available than office space. But, *insomma*, things do look promising.

Sandwich suspense

Lunch at Lola's is a true taste of Tuscan theatre. Every day for the better part of a year my colleagues and I have squeezed in the door at half past twelve in efforts to beat our neighbors to the corner table. The menu is written on a paper place-mat and hung on the wall weekly, but if we all order different things Lola scolds us for bringing confusion to her brain.

Food in Italy always brings about some sort of debate. Now that it's summer Giovanni has taken to ordering an ice-cream sandwich every day after lunch. Half is chocolate and the other half's vanilla. There is always suspense at the table before he tears open the wrapper. If he opens it on the chocolate side, it is destined to be a good day. Vanilla first brings bad luck. After three weeks of continued dessert-induced suspense, I finally asked him. 'If you want to eat the other side first, why don't you just flip the ice-cream around?'

'*Flip it around*?', my colleague asked, appalled by the suggestion. You can't manipulate *il destino* like that!'

'Giovanni, it's not destiny. It's an ice-cream sandwich.'

'See!' he said, slapping his hand on his knee. 'This is where I see you are American. Flip the *gelato*! That would go against Italian fatalistic principles. You Americans are always convinced you have the power to make a situation come out the way you want. You think you have control over the current of life's events!'

'No. What I *think* is that you are completely neurotic and should limit your caffeine intake.' My friend laughed. Odd as the conversation was, it was destined to become odder before our coffee was through. 'Well, at least tell me why "vanilla first brings bad luck?"' I wanted to know. 'Because I like vanilla better and would prefer to eat it last.' Everyone else at the table agreed. It's always best to finish with one's favorite.

'Actually, I always start with my best flavor', I mused.

'It must be an American thing. You come from the society of instant gratification. You want what you want and you want it *fast*', Giovanni told me.

'Yes, and what I want right now is to kick you in the shins. Stop taking every word I say and making it into a cultural study on the American mentality!'

'Look who's talking! You can dish it out but, you can't take it, little Miss Italian Language and Culture.'

I frowned. 'Are you being mean to me on purpose or are you doing it by accident?', I asked

Giovanni was genuinely surprised. 'Mean to you? I'm not being mean to you! *Ti prendo in giro*. If I didn't tease you a bit, you'd never know how deeply I love you.'

Intercultural relationships are never easy. But somehow, we seemed to be having a particularly difficult day. There are several elements of this exchange that I find worthy of discussion. But first thing's first. For those who are wondering, Giovanni does not, in fact, 'love me deeply'. At best, he thinks I'm smart. At worst, he thinks I'm a pain in the neck. The feeling, of course, is mutual. Another day, I would make sure to inform him that English-speaking men would risk their inheritance if they declared 'deep love' to a lady-colleague on lunch break. Right then, though, I wanted to talk about teasing.

'Listen, Deep Love', I told my friend, 'Don't *prendermi in giro* too much. I'd much rather love you than fight you.'

'Oh Linda, sometimes you are quite slow to understand', Giovanni sighed. 'In Italy, when we tease a person, it means we hold them in high regard. We consider them smart enough to capture the core of the joke. Intelligent people can always face themselves without offence.'

An entirely Italian concept, I found his reasoning quite profound and it got my mind ticking. If translated literally, the expression *ti prendo in giro* can be translated as 'I take you around', which to me, sounds like an invitation to see the city. It is an invitation in a way but, the landscape you'll be taken to see may surprise you. *Ti prendo in giro* implies a free tour of the true you. Let your enemies be false to your face and tell you your talents. In Italy, trust your friends to tattle your truths. *Ti prendo in giro* means they are going to take you sight-seeing, but your weaknesses will be the monuments you'll be forced to visit. Admittedly, it's a bit of a torturous trip at first, but it can prove quite worthwhile once you get the hang of it. Italians tease mercilessly. The more merciless the *giro* the deeper the bond.

'Okay, Giova', I sigh, 'Let's pretend I get your point. Teasing is a form of high regard. *Va bene*, fine, I believe you. What I *can't* believe is that you order chocolate ice-cream every day when you don't even like it. Why not choose the sandwich that has only vanilla?'

'And miss out on the suspense? Suspense is much more pleasurable than ice-cream, Linda, and if you'd open your mind, you'd know that.'

'Let's make a deal, Giovanni. I'll open my mind if you shut your mouth.'

My colleague smiled. He loves it when I'm mean to him.

In Italy, it's just more proof of 'loving deeply'.

'Sofia mia'

It was an eerily sunny day and my friend Silvia and I were weaving our way to the park with the greenhouse. Her daughter Sofia had a play date and we were, of course, late. As we dragged the poor child by the cuff through the whizzing traffic of via Bolognese, Sofia made a comment that caught both her mother and I off guard.

'Fosca is Davide's girl', she said in her out-of-the-blue three-year-old way, 'I'm Nico's girl.'

And Nico's girl she was. Upon arrival, the little rogue took her by the hand and sang her a very lengthy on-the-spot serenade. With barely two years of speech under his belt, Nico's sing-song was simple and quite profound. Its only words were 'my Sofia, my Sofia, my Sofia.' By the tenth *Sofia mia* I gave her mother a questioning look. '*Hanno un feeling*', she explained.

'*Un feeling*? This is more than a feeling. This is true love.'

'Oh, Linda, let the child at least turn four', Silvia laughed.

'I don't know', I countered, 'considering how long it takes for the average Italian to actually pop the question, they'd best start their eternal courtship now. Especially if they have *un feeling*.

As it turns out the expression *avere un feeling* does not necessarily mean you've fallen in love; it simply means that you get on well with someone. English speakers, who talk about sentiments as if they were describing electrical equipment, would probably say something like 'he and I really click' or we have a connection.' Both 'click' and 'connection' allude to the Anglo's technological view of well-functioning friendship. Solid relationships 'work', shaky ones 'stop working.' It's simply a question of mechanics. You've got to manipulate the rapport until you hear 'a click.' Only then will the emotional mechanisms start functioning with some level of reliability.

But if household appliances leave you cold, another adequate translation for *avere un feeling* is the well-loved English phrase 'to have chemistry.' Let's just say that when sparks fly or personal intuition meets instant understanding, there's undoubtedly *un feeling* floating around in the stratosphere. But those who favor steadfast science over fleeting indefinable sentiment should still refrain from translating literally. In Italian, *abbiamo chimica* is nothing more than a hallway warning to a classmate who's late for a lecture on molecular theorems.

Funnily enough, few Italians realize that in English the expression 'have a feeling' has more to do with harboring a sneaking suspicion than it does with nurturing empathy toward someone you're keen on. In English, if you say 'I have a feeling about Marcello' it means you've got a hunch about him.

A far cry from chemistry, this type of linguistic confusion often runs rampant in Italy. Italians are not die-hard word nationalists and they employ foreign expression with the zeal of those who love to speak—no matter the tongue. Words like 'computer', 'weekend', 'stop' and dozens of others have quickly become an ever-present part of daily chatter. Original meanings and structures often get changed as soon as they pull into the Italian port.

The straightforward noun 'foot' grows into 'footing'—the pseudo-English equivalent to jogging. The leisure activity 'camping' becomes the universally recognized synonym for 'camp-site.' Italians say 'spot' to mean 'television commercial' and 'beauty' to say 'cosmetics case.' All this is proof that Italy is fertile soil: sow even the simplest of English expressions into this ground and what sprouts is a strange new species whose significance scarcely resembles the original seed.

'Maybe Italians change meanings because we are not very good at defining things', Silvia told me. 'It's also more fun to leave space for open interpretation', she mused as we watched the soulmates play in the sandbox. Nico was singing again.

'In English, we would call their feeling 'a first crush', I said.

'"Crush"?', Silvia asked. 'Is that like "crash"?'

I laughed, 'No, it's more like "smash".'

'Oh. How ugly', my friend frowned. '*Un feeling* sounds much more beautiful.'

Unsurprised, I smile. Leave it to the Italians to import only the beautiful words for love.

An 'allora' man

It's Monday night and as usual I'm desperate for a word. The rest of the world is out watching summer soccer matches on the big screen in piazza Indipendenza. Italy is playing tonight and everyone else knows the word they are looking for. If they find it, I will hear 'goal' yelled from all open windows. Nice as that would be, the word I need still escapes me.

In Italy, when a person has no idea what to say, they usually start with *allora*. It buys time. So that's what I'm going to start with tonight. It's as good an expression as any I suppose. Better than most, actually. Most words move within strict boundaries of meaning.

Allora is well-versed on versatility. Adaptable as water, it conforms itself to almost any scenario.

The dictionary will tell you that *allora* means 'so' or 'thus', but, in reality, the meaning of the word depends on who you are and how you say it. In Italy, when a teacher yells '*Allora*!' it means you'd better sit up and shut up. Trouble's a-coming. Either find a way to stop Carlo Sassetti from swinging on the shutters or be quick and close the window. The woman means business. There is a certain power in the expression, especially when it's accompanied by an exclamation point. *Allora* followed by a comma, however, changes the cards completely. Relax. Her monologue is going to be long. Hours may pass before you'll be asked to look lively again.

When the neighbor lady says *allora* it's usually accompanied by a question mark. Your mother has most likely told her all the gory details. She has already been adequately briefed on your personal saga and has taken it upon herself to rearrange your story upside-down and backwards. All the *signora* needs now is just a bit more spice to make the batter come out right. '*Allora*?', she smiles as

you come up the steps. What she means is 'cut to the chase.' She knows you're in love; what she wants is the wedding date.

When your colleague says *allora*, it means your meeting might actually start going somewhere. Put your ears back on and start listening again, a plausible explanation may be provided. In work situations, *allora* is great for gathering evidence. It gives you time to gather your chips before you place your bet on a risky hand.

My grandfather was an artisan and an *allora* man. He had the wonderful habit of talking to me as if we were always in the midst of a very important conversation. Ours was an ongoing dialogue that started soon after I was born and just continued on and on until the sun set on his days. *Allora bimba*, he would say, whenever we met, as if he was just about to reach the conclusion of a discussion we had started six months earlier. He would always greet me with *allora*, like someone who was just getting to the good part of the story. I've never thought about it before now, but for him, the word was a bridge across time.

For my grandfather *allora* served innumerable purposes. It was 'let's see now' and 'let's get to the bottom of this.' *Allora* was 'what do you think?', and 'where do we go from here?' *Allora* was what he said every time he sat on his stool to make a new mirror. It was a word the man used to collect his strength, the prelude to all creative effort. But it was also the culmination of a job that pleased him. Once he finished his etching, he would hold the mirror up for me to see. '*Allora*, tell me, is the work to your liking?' Mostly he etched ladies and gents from the seventeenth century, falling in love under a cherry tree. The work was always to my liking.

My grandmother died last week, almost 20 years after her husband. Perhaps this spring they will find a nice new tree to fall in love under. Perhaps they will have the chance to continue a conversation they had started years ago. If they meet again, he will greet her with *allora*. I'm sure of it.

The say-do difference

In October, Martina and I piled into an already crowded café in hope of a corner table. Once a month we met there to talk, sip *cappuccino*, and perhaps jot a line or two in our 'be bohemian' notebooks. We were actually both quite busily writing when someone at the bar burst suddenly into flames. Not literally of course, but it's the best way to describe the explosive verbal exchange that occurred when the barman served up a lukewarm *cappuccio* that the customer called 'cold.'

As soon as the barman offered to restore world peace by providing another cup, the customer stepped back, took his final sip, and said. 'No, no. It's not necessary. *Si fa per dire.*' With that, he turned and headed for the door, restoring all semblance of placidity in the place. The *barista*, entirely unmoved by the episode, quickly collected the cup and saucer from the counter-top and went back to his task.

I sat watching the exchange with some measure of fascination. In English, complaining is a catalyst for change. If you're an English speaker and you tell the barman that your *cappuccino* is cold, it means you're intent on getting another cup. In English, we talk in hopes of making things happen. In Italian, you make things happen so you can talk about them. This guy didn't want a refill—catching the mistake was gratification enough.

And that's where the phrase *si fa per dire* comes into play.

Translated literally as 'one does so that one may say', it's often used as 'Oh, never mind, I just thought you should know.' A tell-tale Italian expression, *si fa per dire* expresses unconformity and magnanimity at the same time 'You're wrong and I want the world to know it—but don't worry about fixing the mess. The cleaners are coming tomorrow.'

For me, the phrase illustrates the inborn Italian ability to overlook trite daily inadequacies. In Italy, it's essential that the culprit admit the error of his ways, but there is no real desire to punish the perpetrator. In this country, it's the confession that counts. Once that's over with, it's best to leave people to their business.

'Martina, why do you think Italians make such a show of protesting over things they don't really care about?'

'They care; they just don't expect their protests to produce immediate effects.'

'In English, complaints are always a means to an end.'

'Not here.' My friend thought. 'Maybe it's because Italians have quite a feminine psyche.'

'What do you mean?'

'It's like what psychologists say. Women speak to find understanding. If a woman complains that it's raining, she simply wants you to understand that she's getting wet. She doesn't want you to run for an umbrella necessarily. Men never quite get that. Her goal is not to solve the problem, but to share it. The same is true for Italians. They speak to share the pain and glory, not in hopes of achieving results.'

'So you think English speakers think more like men do?'

'Maybe in a way', she mused. 'In English, speech is about problem solving. The driving force behind a gripe is the idea that "something must be done." Italians prefer the filibuster—talk an issue to death so that nothing whatsoever will be done about it.'

The thought struck us both as immensely funny, and Martina and I interrupted our laughter only long enough to order two hot chocolates from our already disapproving waiter. He met our request with reluctance. Couldn't we see that it was too early in the year for hot chocolate? With the sun as hot as it was, we should know better than to rush the season.

I greeted his grimace with ruffled feathers. 'So, does all this mean you can't make it for us?

'Of course we can make it', he said with surprise. '*Si fa per dire.*'

Right.

How quickly one forgets. In Italy, inappropriate choices must be disputed at all costs. Light must be shed on suspicious behaviors. But no worries. Around here, chocolate sins are very readily forgiven.

La, la, la

Although Italy has taught me to nurture a neurotic need for aesthetic perfection, I am not much of a scenery girl. And, while I do prefer palaces to skyscrapers, I'm seldom subject to the wide-eyed 'wow' that gives weak knees to those who marvel at Tuscan hillsides and fifteenth-century cityscape. The fact that I was born without a sense of direction probably contributes to my lack of landscape-based enthusiasm. I can pass the same building three times in 10 minutes without realizing that I'm retracing my steps. In fact, I can *live* in the same building for three years and not know how to get there from the freeway exit.

For many, Italy's seductive powers lie in the physical beauty of her landscape, the curve of her geography and the color of her frescos. My own infatuation for this country is primarily auditory. The buzz of a crowded café, the sound of high heels on cobblestone and even the screech of skidding Vespas somehow profoundly speak to me. Italy's language fills the air with a lightness and humor I have not found elsewhere. Its supple flexibility, the versatility of its vocabulary and the sheer variability of its dialects enchant me. In a word, I'm a word-geek and Italy is the end-all and be-all.

This country has six definite articles. *Il-lo-la-i-gli-le.* Even those who do not normally swoon at the sound of syllables have to admit that people who invented six ways to say 'the' make great conversation partners. To me, *il-lo-la-i-gli-le* works like Supercalifragilisticexpialidocious.

It is mind-chocolate that stimulates the 'be-happy' gene. First graders sing it on the bus and who can help by hum along?

But show tunes aside, definite articles are definitely worth their weight in gold. Earn yourself one and you've got it made. To use an article when referring to a friend or foe is a hard-won sign of

ITALIAN VOICE LESSONS

...le, la, lo, iiiiii...

belonging. It means you're considered part of the group—a state that is essential to survival in Italy. For men, the article *il* always proceeds a nickname, and it is a banner to familiarity; Matteo becomes *il* Teo, Leonardo is *il* Leo and Niccolò is known as *il* Nico. Women, on the other hand, can be awarded a *la* without need to shorten their names. In the country that gave rise to leaders like the Magnificent, the Elder and the Gouty, there is something slightly dizzying about hearing yourself referred to as 'The Linda.' The principle is simple: once they love you, your name becomes a superlative adjective. The tallest, the fattest, the best, the worst, the most original. The most unforgettable, irreparable you.

On Saturday, we went to have lunch at the Badiani house in the hills near Prato.

It was our company party, because countryside soirees are exempt from party taxes. The sun was setting and a few of us sat in a line on a stone wall overlooking the valley.

'I don't think I've ever seen anything so beautiful', I sighed.

Marco nudged Giovanni, who was sitting on his other side. 'She says that every time she comes. When it comes to scenery, she is like a goldfish. No long-term memory.'

'He's right', I admitted.

'Well, you sure remember every damn word *I* say. And you always make me look like the village idiot.'

I moved to respond, but Marco was faster. 'Sorry for you, Giova, but La Linda writes non-fiction.'

We all laughed together at his joke, but I was happiest. I had somehow earned a definite article. *Il-lo-la-i-gli-le. Le-gli-i-lo-la-il.* Yes, Tuscany is beautiful—the hills at dusk, the dusty green of olive groves, high Sangiovese vines and all that landscape jazz. Still—it's the *la* that rings as real music to me.

The Red Room

Vincenzo had the unsmiling face of a bureaucrat, but he was actually quite likeable once he decided you were tolerable. As an employee of the Municipality of Florence, he needed to learn English for when he was asked to officiate foreign weddings in Palazzo Vecchio's Red Room. Despite his slightly cerebral countenance, I liked him right away. He came to his lesson on time and was willing to share his ballpoint pens and his historical knowledge—two essential areas in which I am always miserably lacking.

Vincenzo's English skills were quite good, if you didn't count the Italianisms he never managed to weed out of the language. Most students groan when you tell them things like 'in English, we don't use the present simple to talk about the present tense.' But Vincenzo knew enough about both languages to delight in their quirks. He always reacted to sad truths with an expression of thoughtful surprise—*figurati*.

Vincenzo's favorite brand of *figurati* can be translated as 'Imagine that!' but like many Italian words, the expression has multiple meanings. It's often used as 'of course' and serves as a humble form of 'you're welcome.' When you want to say 'I can't figure out what I've done to deserve your gratitude', you opt for *figurati*. My student used the phase with a frequency that I found nothing short of exhilarating. The word worked everywhere, like parsley.

The other day as we were finishing up a listening exercise and Vincenzo made me an unexpected proposal.

'Linda, can you be free today at five?', he asked me.

'Yes, why?'

'An American couple is getting married in the Red Room—they need a maid of honor.'

'*Figurati*! Had I known "bridesmaid" was a profession I wouldn't have studied languages.'

Vincenzo smiled, 'The ceremony lasts 20 minutes and you need to bring your passport and a bouquet of flowers. I can give you 50 euro per wedding.'

'Great, thanks.'

'*Figurati*. Thank *you*.'

Fifty euro for signing a 'Married in Florence' parchment! I would have done it for free, of course. Vincenzo didn't know it, but I happen to have a real weakness for love-based ceremonies. As a child, I'd force my cousin Leonardo to marry me on a daily basis. I did it for the lace veil and plastic flowers. I don't quite remember what his reasons were, but it's highly likely that I gave him no choice in the matter. Venice in June is a rather fashionable place to celebrate nuptials, even for six-year-olds. Even the Doge officially married the city every year by throwing a ring into the canal. And he had his palace built to look like a wedding cake. So, I was not alone in my thinking.

I met Vincenzo in the courtyard of city hall at 4:45. He was wearing his official red, white and green sash and made a good stand-in for the mayor. Our American love-birds, both wearing white, showed up without a single guest. This worried Vincenzo considerably. In Italy, it's illegal to tie the knot without at least two witnesses. Barely 10 minutes before the start of the ceremony, my student took me under the arm as if we were the ones about to say vows and led me into the street in search of at least one more willing wedding guest.

An older couple carrying grocery bags passed the entrance of the Comune and my officiant lost no time with formalities. 'We're celebrating a wedding in five minutes', he told them 'Can you come to the ceremony? We need more witnesses.'

The man didn't even blink. 'We have frozen vegetables with us', he said, 'They'll thaw.' Contrary to popular belief Italians are a very practical people who are good at taking things in stride. We might have been asking him what time it was.

'*Figurati*, if spinach matters, Gianmario', the lady scolded her husband. '*Su, via*, let's help these people.'

The ceremony was simple and quite beautiful in an 'imagine that' sort of way. The couple promised to love each other forever and to 'educate all offspring according to their talents and abilities' as per article 144 of the Italian Constitution. The bride and groom treated their wedding party of strangers to *prosecco* after the ceremony and then left the spinach man and his wife to salvage what was left of their thawing veggies.

Once bid a huggable American good-bye, Vincenzo and I were left at the bar with the beginnings of the early *aperitivo* crowd.

'It must be nice to marry people for a living', I mused.

'Yes—it renews one's faith in the continuity of life.'

'And confirms the utter weirdness of it.'

'Definitely. Are you happy to have caught the bouquet?'

'*Figurati*. There are pluses to being the only one in the line-up.'

'Right', he smiled. 'That's what I figured.'

The dead bridge

I have just spent the entire afternoon dumping the contents of my drawers into cardboard boxes. I found them crushed on aisle seven at the Coop supermarket this morning and spent the better part of an hour trying to tape them into squares again. Now that the boxes are almost full, I am terrified that the bottoms will burst before I cross the threshold of my new flat. The later it gets the more this strikes me as a legitimate worry, because, alas, I am only an optimist in the morning.

Fortunately, George Gershwin has kept me company as I've packed, acting as a musical buffer to my mounting sense of paranoia. Still—if I do succeed in lugging these items across Florence unharmed, where will I put them once I get there? My new apartment was advertised as a *bilocale* but, in all honesty, the second room amounts to what English speakers would call a 'linen closet.' A real closet is, of course, no where to be found. Thus I've also dedicated a substantial dose of worry to how we'll fit the wardrobe into an unwilling Fiat Punto.

Packing day was not all bad, of course. The sound of rain outside did offer me some comfort. There's nothing like a Sunday storm for sifting through one's life to see what needs to be kept and what ought to be thrown away. Admittedly, most of the things I should throw away, I'm definitely keeping. According to experts, the packrat tendency to hoard useless paraphernalia with the vague intention of possibly using it one day is a bad sign. It connotes an obsession with death, they say.

I'm not too worried though. Death is on everyone's mind this weekend, because *i morti*—Italy's favorite excuse for a three-day get-away—is right around the corner. In Italy, the November 1 bank holiday is officially accredited to the saints, but it's the 'dead' who get all the glory for the long weekend. The saints, though, don't seem to mind the slight and continue to smile sweetly upon us. This year, they've squeezed their shared celebration into a lucky square labeled 'Wednesday.' '*Dove vai per i morti*? Where are you going for the dead?', is currently the question of choice, as half the country prepares to abandon their posts for a bit of temporary rest in peace. Fortunately, 'the dead' they are discussing have little to do with deceased ancestors and much to do with living it up at a mountain retreat. Chestnuts and bread-based stews abound, as friends gather in country homes to make the best of the long weekend.

My neo-landlord, worried my move would kill his 'dead plans' suggested I make appropriate provisions, 'It would be best if you transfer yourself before November', he said. 'Because I'm going to

Garfagnana for *il ponte dei morti.*'

He is not the only one. During this *ponte*, or 'bridge', schools close, businesses pull down the padlock, families pack up—the whole country turns construction worker in efforts to mount improvised scaffolding across the chasm that divides work and play.

The Italian calendar is, in fact, full of 'bridges.' The next one will stretch over the weekend of December 8. According to my date-book calculations, this year festivities for the Immaculate Conception fall on a Friday—another happy coincidence for *ponte* people everywhere.

Although Italians are not very apt to consult their watches, they are quite prone to checking their calendars. This chronological trend is quite easily explained because, unlike English speakers, Italians perceive time in months rather than minutes. This tendency could be due to the eons it takes to actually do anything in this country. Italy's ballooning bureaucracy and cinched economy are often cited as common culprits for slowing down the way the country calculates time. But it could just be that Italians prefer calendars to ticking clocks out of gratitude to Caesar. After all, it was he who created the Western calendar, back in the days when Italy ruled the world. For the Italian, that's still the time-line that counts, no matter what modern man insists on tying to his wrist.

I know I've said this before, but it's always reassuring to remember Rome. For anyone pursuing 'real life' in Italy, frequent thoughts of Roman grandeur are an essential coping mechanism—especially during a move. It's well-known that house painters, expert electricians, Internet technicians and anyone hired by the phone company are particularly dependent on month-based chronology. 'Be patient', my well-meaning landlord told me yesterday, 'after the *ponte*, you will be able to get settled with higher speed.'

It's a pre-Christmas exodus that many Florentines plan for in advance.

'Right', I frowned.

Undaunted by my grimace, he laughed, 'It's not too long of a wait, Linda, considering how many of the living have to come back from 'the dead.'

I smile. The man is good with puns—a quality I hold in highest regard. Perhaps I can, in fact, be patient.

Control issues

A month after I had settled into my new apartment, my ex-landlady called. She had just received a notice in the mail from the garbage collectors. They had neglected to bill our neighborhood for three years and now that they'd finally gotten around to it, I was expected to pay for 36 months of service by mid-December.

'I thought I'd let you know', she told me, 'but if I were you, I wouldn't pay it. Just pretend you're foreign and that you can't read the bill.'

'Technically, I'm not foreign. I have an Italian passport', I replied.

'If *un controllo* arrives you'll have to pay up immediately, including the fine. But Lord knows, they're disorganized. It would take them months to find you. Unless you have residency papers at your new place. Still—you should be fine, unless *arriva un controllo*.'

Italians are always very conscious that a 'control squad' could someday appear out of nowhere and hold them responsible for all their past and future fudging. Fear of *un controllo* is virtually the only reason people are pushed to pay the majority of what they owe. My ex-landlady is a frail, 88-year-old noblewoman with the mind of a sharp 18-year-old. Still, she was talking like we were wrapped up in some sort of lurid scam, and I was feeling guilty already.

I've often argued that Italians do not foster the same self-induced sense of guilt that plagues Anglo cultures. As Giorgio Moro says, 'In Italy, we don't feel guilty, we just *are* guilty.' In other words, if a fraud squad were to suddenly knock on people's doors in search of 'proper paperwork', half the country would be obliged to kneel on their doorsteps and beg for political asylum.

Have you avoided the TV tax by claiming you don't have a television? Have you signed a contract that says you work fewer hours than you actually do? Have you strengthened your roof rafters without permission from the City Building Committee? Have you paid the doctor in cash to have him move your urgent appointment forward?

Yeah, well, so has everyone else. In Italy, there's not enough time and certainly not enough money to do things the 'right' way. Public opinion is quasi unanimous: daily survival is hard, even for the fittest. We're taxed on everything, including the kitchen sink. Red-tape abounds in this country and it exists everywhere except between the sand and the seashore. Its bureaucratic maze is quite a challenge and, admittedly, it may take a little side-stepping to escape the Minotaur. Thus, any efforts to successfully chop hassles in half should be congratulated rather than criminalized.

The morning after my landlady's news I called Giorgio Moro in Milan. He was at a fair for electrical engineers and I was sure my phone call would constitute much of the day's excitement.

'Why does everyone fear '*un controllo*'?', I asked my friend.

'Well, good morning to you too. *Un controllo*? What happened?'

'Nothing. Nobody's paid the garbage tax for three years and I'm wondering if I should feel threatened. Do *controlli* actually happen in real life, or is it just a case of collective paranoia?'

'Maybe, it's a fear left over from Fascism', he said. 'Or maybe we worry because we're all guilty of trying to beat the system. But don't worry about the garbage tax—in all other ways you're a perfectly respectable citizen. In fact, they might even arrest you for that.'

'Giorgio, I've been waiting years for some sort of *controllo* to actually arrive.'

He laughed, 'You want them to declare you Hopelessly Legal?

'Yes. I want someone somewhere to study my tax forms and commend my legality.'

'Well, why didn't you say so? I commend your legality.'

'No, I want it officially printed on stamped paper.'

'Okay', Giorgio agreed, 'but I may have to blackmail someone to get you the stamp.'

'Never mind. In cahoots with you, they'd surely find something wrong with me. How's the fair?'

'Good. Just pray that *un controllo* doesn't arrive. They'd close it down in all of five minutes.'

'The pavilion people haven't paid the garbage tax either?'

'Garbage is nothing, compared to the garbage that goes on in this place.'

'Giorgio Moro, you'd better be good.'

'I have no choice. Unfortunately, I happen to have constant personal *controllo*. Namely you.'

I smile. 'There is no way I'm paying by mid-December.'

'I know. You're gonna wait until January 1st.'

'I was thinking more along the lines of the Befana, on the sixth.'

'Done deal, Befana', he said.

The man was comparing me to an old hag with a wart on her nose and the garbage men were coming after me. But I take it with a grain of salt. It's called learning to survive in Italy.

Recommendations

In 1998, I was hired to teach English at the military barracks in the province of Mantova. The course was funded by the European community so that all the draft soldiers would be able to understand each other. The post was extraordinarily well paid if you have no aversion to 18-year-olds, who—remarkably—don't recall ever having seen a woman before.

Probably the most challenging experience of my language-teaching career, that course had all the makings of a top-notch mentor movie. There was the shepherd's son from Sardegna who didn't know how to read and the brilliant but angry boy who was destined to lose a big fight or win a huge prize one day. And then, there was the poor but clean kid who was really going to make something of himself. That was Raffaele, my favorite. And yes, the fact that I had a pet proves that I wasn't cut out to star in a super-teacher flick. It was a pity. With a more suitable tutor, those boys would have been a blockbuster cast. As it was, all they got was a seven-hour-a-day, month-long English course with a woman who wanted them to march to the rhythm of irregular verbs.

For the first week, at least, I was Mrs. Rottenmeier incarnate. No swearing, no smoking and no paper airplanes unless they were flying 500-word essays in English. Surprisingly enough, it was the first real taste of discipline they'd had since being drafted into the Italian army. I clung to the 'firm but fair' principle with sweaty palms and planted my feet like a toy-soldier half buried in sand. No one was going to knock me down, not even men in uniform.

The boys understood me faster than they understood English. By day three, they dropped their innuendos and decided I fit into the feisty 'watch-your-mouth' category usually occupied by mothers and sisters. And that's when they decided to adopt me.

The adoption option is a common alternative for Italian men who have abandoned all hope of seducing you. If all else fails, turn paternal: women who won't be ruined need to be protected.

We climbed the rungs of mutual affection quickly, as often happens when you're forced to spend innumerable hours of suffering in someone's constant company. I taught them the royal order of adjectives; they taught me both *briscola* and *scopa*, two games you play with a deck of cards from Treviso. Their inability to master word order frustrated me. My ability to make a mess of every hand dealt to me fascinated them.

I brought them treats twice a week and they took turns accompanying me to the gate—a trade I definitely considered worth the baking. If I was escorted across the facility, the staring stopped. Their body language expressed an unspoken code: 'No gawking at the English teacher, bud. This girl's a lady.'

My young adoptive 'fathers' were very concerned about a whole series of issues that usually only bother body-guards. Did I go out alone and walk by myself at night? Did I leave the shutters closed if I left for the weekend? Did I know that the Big Bad Wolf sometimes dresses as grandma?

'*Mi raccomando*, Prof, be careful', they'd say. 'Be sure you take a taxi home, *mi raccomando*.' 'Turn your key three times, *mi raccomando*.'

A strange combination of 'take care' and 'be careful', what sounds a lot like 'recommend' is actually closer to 'urge' or 'beg.'

Mi raccomando is what mothers say to make sure you'll actually keep your promises. It eases the doubt that you weren't really listening and anchors off-handed commitments: 'You *will* do it, won't you?' The use of 'mi' is what clinches the deal: it implies that the request should be considered a personal favor. 'Take care of this, please, as a favor to me.' That tiny reflexive pronoun carries the weight of the warning. *Mi* is the seed of guilt—you'll hurt someone's feelings if you don't comply. Still, there is comfort in the insistence with which Italians use the phrase. I loved hearing the boys' admonitions. *Mi raccomando* somehow made us responsible to each other.

On Monday of week four, I showed up for class and found that all the desks were empty. Milosevic had gone crazy and the boys had been called on a peace-keeping mission in Kosovo in support of UN troops. The cadets were gone, the course had been cancelled and no one had thought to tell the teacher. Europe had decided it was time for my pupils to use English on the battlefield.

Two armed guards accompanied me to the gate, and on the grounds there were only new soldiers who had yet to be trained not to stare. I walked, wishing I'd taught my students something useful.

The royal order of adjectives is worth nothing in a world where things get turned upside-down so quickly.

As we approached the exit, I saw Raffaele striding towards me. There was a difference in his step as if some unfamiliar soldier had suddenly borrowed his boots.

'You didn't go with the rest of them?', I asked.

'Not yet. I'm leaving Friday.'

I know I should have thought of something profoundly inspiring to say at that point, but like I said, I wasn't made for mentor movies.

'Good God, Raffaele, don't go and get yourself killed', I told him. He gave me a sad smile.

'I'll do my best, Miss Linda. And you remember to practice your game. Whatever you do—hold onto the threes—and *settebello*, those win in *scopa, mi raccomando.*'

He grinned, his sadness gone, and saluted me instead of saying good-bye. And then he turned and walked away.

'Be safe', I whispered, watching him go. '*Mi raccomando. Mi raccomando. Mi raccomando.*'

'Italiani mammoni'

Giorgio Moro was admittedly very relieved to be walking me home. The night had been a terrible bore, he said. Unfortunately, I couldn't really deny it. I had spent our entire dinner picking his brain for an Italian expression that might please me. Deadline was just two days away. 'Too much to say' or 'not enough to say' were my blanket objections to every phase he had mentioned over the course of the evening. Luckily, Giorgio has been my friend since birth and is absolutely undaunted by my lifelong unwillingness to cooperate.

'Hey, why don't you write something about *Italiani mammoni*. That's a good saying', he said.

'Giorgio, I know you're trying to be helpful. But frankly, the Italian man's reluctance to sever the umbilical cord is an exhausting topic, even on a day when I'm not this cranky.'

'Exhausting? Why?',

'Because if I write about *Italiani mammoni*, I'll end up whining that the whole country is populated with inept men still live at home until their late 30s or have their mothers come over weekly to dust their flats and fill their refrigerators.'

'Twice a week, actually.'

'Giorgio! Do you really want to be known as the man who takes laundry to his mother's on Friday and expects it pressed before roast duck dinner on Sunday?'

'She *wants* to do that, Linda.'

'Yes, but the fact that you let her makes me forget all of your redeeming qualities.'

Giorgio laughed. '*Ti voglio bene*, is that not redeeming enough?'

'Maybe.' I said doubtfully.

'*And* if you don't come up with an article this week, I will *still* love you.'

'Really? Okay then, you're redeemed.'

Giorgio Moro smiled, glad to have at least one point in his favor. Then he kissed me goodnight on the top of my head like my father used to do and told me not to think about Italian mothers or their sons until morning.

It was, of course, very sound advice. And as often happens with great advice, I made no effort whatsoever to follow it. Unfortunately for me, I find night the best time to think about things that make no sense when the sun's up. There was no way I could sleep with so many mysteries to solve. Why are Italian men such incurable 'mom-ers?' Why is this country so plagued with nationwide filial co-dependence? And how could I possibly write an article on something so excruciatingly difficult to justify?

Especially if I was allowed only 750 words.

I would need at least 10 times that to even touch the iceberg of Italian oedipal tendencies. Honestly, what good were 750 measly words to explain the brand of love that binds mothers and sons in Italy? 'Giorgio Moro and his bright ideas', I grumbled, 'Lucky for him he loves me. Otherwise he'd be in real trouble for having suggested something so difficult.'

And that's when it came. The answer, I mean. Thinking about mothers and sons and love and Giorgio all in one breath brought me the answer—or at least the beginning of one. Find out how a country loves and you'll find the solution to all its pathologies. I

In Italy, you see, there are two main ways to love someone, and surprisingly these categories are quite clear cut. Lovers own the phrase *ti amo*, while family and friends use the phrase *ti voglio bene*. It still means 'I love you' but translates as 'I want you well.' In other words, *ti voglio bene* is love made manifest. 'I want you well and that is all. I want your life to be painless and your stomach to be full. I want your road to be paved, your house to be clean and your dreams to be safe. Your happiness will become my reward. So let me be your 'Giving Tree'. Sit in my shade and eat my apples. Cut me down and burn my branches. I want you warm. I want you well.'

Could this view of family-love be behind the *italiani mammoni* phenomenon? It was just a thought, but I was suddenly willing to bet on it. Or a least sleep on it. 'Maybe tomorrow I will run the idea by Giorgio Moro', I told myself. 'Hell, maybe tomorrow I'll run the idea by everyone.'

With that, I switched off the light and lay there in the darkness with an unexpected feeling of hope surging out of nowhere. Maybe it was simply the first time I'd ever realized the beauty of *ti voglio bene*. Or maybe I had really cracked the code. Either way, it's kind of nice to fall asleep thinking that love is the answer.

Acknowledgements

To those who peer out from between these pages.
To those who peer into their world with delight.
To those who turned this small slice of life into a real-live book.
And to those who, ultimately, believe in roses.

My heartfelt thanks.

Linda Falcone

Linda Falcone is a language teacher who loves the rhythm of irregular verbs as much as the sound of rain on the roof. Born in northern California and raised in a bi-cultural family, she is currently celebrating fifteen years of permanent Italian living. She believes in full amphitheatres in spring, empty beaches in autumn and newspaper articles year-round that reek of fresh ink and speak of loveliness. In 2008, after two years of writing 'Italian Voices', Falcone began her second column in *The Florentine*, 'Where Beauty is Fact: Moments from Everyday Italy'. Local readers quickly christened the column, *Il fatto bello della settimana* and the name stuck as the only Italian title in Florence's English-speaking newspaper. Falcone's first collection of vignettes, *Italians Dance and I'm a Wallflower*—a tongue-in-cheek ode to Italian language and customs—led the way to *If They are Roses*, her second book.

Leo Cardini is a Florentine artist of few words and many mediums—acrylics, graphics, comics, play-dough and snow. He believes in pine trees weighed down with white and stadiums filled with people wearing purple. Given the chance, he'll illustrate pew missals to keep all the kids wide-eyed and quiet at church. Partner in *Agile Logica* graphic design studio since 2000 and *The Florentine Press* since 2004, his drawings arrive late and dishevelled—sometimes off-beat—and always in search of a smile.

THE ✤ FLORENTINE

The Florentine is a bi-weekly newspaper for the English-speaking community of Florence, Italy, including residents, students, visiting professionals, and tourists. With an international editorial staff and over 200 contributing writers from around the globe, it is the most widely read English paper in Florence and reaches subscribers world-wide.

Serving online subscribers to *The Florentine*, www.theflorentine.net also features the current issue of the paper and upcoming events in and around Florence, as well as a photo repository, blogs, and back issues and an archive of articles from the paper.

The Florentine Press is dedicated to publishing books in English about Florence and Italy, both past and present. From essays to scholarly studies, the books from The Florentine Press explore this rich and vibrant culture, its language, food and wine, arts, history, and terrain. Current titles are available in bookstores in Italy and the United States, and through www.theflorentine.net:

The Florentine — www.theflorentine.net — The Florentine Press
via dei Banchi, 4 - 50123 Florence, Italy
phone +39.055.2306616, fax +39.055.9060996
info@theflorentine.net
www.theflorentine.net

Creative group Agile Logica designs *The Florentine* and the books of The Florentine Press.
www.agilelogica.it